The System of the Dalai Lama Reincarnation

Chen Qingying

China Intercontinental Press

Contents

I.Tibetan Buddhism and the System of Living Buddha Reincarnation

The Living Buddha Reincarnation System as a means of providing for succession among leaders of Tibetan Buddhism is unique to it.

In the 7th century, Buddhism was promoted in Tibet from both India and the Central Plains, as represented by two vivid examples, namely the marriages between Tubo Tsampo (king) Songtsan Gampo and Nepal Princess Bhributi as well as Princess Wencheng of the Tang Dynasty. Both of the two princesses brought a Buddhist figure to the Tubo Kingdom. Princess Bhributi brought an image of the 8-year-old Sakyamuni and Princess Wencheng brought an image of Sakyamuni at 12. These images were set up for worship in the Rampoche Monastery and Jokhang Monastery in Lhasa respectively.

The position of Buddhism gradually became stable with the support of

Potala palace:Residence of the Dalai Lama. CHEN ZONGLIE

the Tubo royal family. At that time, 12 monasteries were established, but they were so small that they contained no monks, only a figure of Buddha. Songtsan Gampo took charge of the translation of many sutras and established laws requiring people to believe in Buddhism, which helped its rapid spread.

In 779, Samye Monastery was established, and became the first to have monks ; seven royal children became monks, which was a significant event in Tibetan Buddhist history.

Some 200 years later, Buddhism enjoyed a fresh revival during the reign of the eighth Tsanpo Rabajun. He stipulated that residents in Tubo give alms and that one member of each family should become a monk and every seven families should support one monk. At the same time, he also invited leading monks and scholars from everywhere to translate the sutras. They translated sutras according to uniform stylistic rules and layout and completed the first Tibetan-Sanskrit dictionary. These actions of the Tsanpo strengthened the power of the monastic groups and aroused the dissatisfaction of followers of the traditional Bon religion. In 841, when the Bon

Statues of songtsan Gambo, Napaless Princess Bhributi and Tang Dynasty Princess Wenchen: In the 7 th Centary, Songtsan Gambo married Napalese Princess Bhributi and Tang Dynasty Princess Wencheng. The three statues are preserved in the Potala palace.　　　　　　　　　　　　　　　　*CHEN ZONGLIE*

<< . . . .
Princess Wencheng (second left)
brought the statue of the 12-year-old
Sakyamuni to Tibet.

CHEN ZONGLIE

adherent Dalhun Weda Nagyian killed Rabajun, and the latter's younger brother, Lang Darma, he assumed power with Bon support. In 843, it was stipulated that all monasteries in Tibet were to be closed, figures of Buddha destroyed and monks forced to return to secular life in posts such as butcher or hunter, and all sutras burned or sealed up. This put an end to the first propagation period of Tibetan Buddhism.

However, Tibetan Buddhism did not die out. Some followers of Buddhism escaped from the central region of Tibet and began to propagate Buddhism in Dokang (Amdo and Kham area) and Ngari. Moreover, they invited some famous monks such as Atisa to help spread the faith. Supported by local political power, these two areas became a remote Buddhist center. Around 970, Tibetan Buddhism entered U-Tsang from Dokang and Ngari, helping launch the second great propagation period of Tibetan Buddhism.

During this time, over 20 sects and branches came into being, with the Nyingma, Gedan, Sagya and Gagyu sects as the four leading ones. Among sects of Tibetan Buddhism, the Nyingma Sect has the longest history, with strong local cultural traits and an emphasis on execration and exorcism. It has loose management and its disciples are decentralized. Under this revival, its major sutras were dug out from their underground hiding places or caves. Until the 16th and 17th century, the Nyingma Sect had its own monasteries, the major ones being Dorjezha Monastery, located near the meeting place of Yarlung Zangbo River and Lhasa River, and Mingzhuling Monastery in Shannan Zhanang County.

Statue of Bribhuti preserved in the Potala Palace.

CHEN ZONGLIE

The Gedan Sect originated from Atisa, whose disciple Zongdainba was its formal founder. In 1055, Zongdainba held a mourning ceremony for Atisa in Nyitang and established a monastery there for preserving his mentorís remains. In 1056, he came to Razheng and established Razheng Monastery, which became the base for the Gedan Sectís development.

The Sagya Sect got its name from its main base, Sagya Monastery. On its walls were painted three-color stripes of red, white and black, which symbolize Wisdom Buddha, Goddess of Meray, and Diamond Buddha. The Sagya Sect has five significant founders. Sapan Gunggar Gyaincain, the fourth founder, played an important role in bringing Tibet and the hinterland together in 13th century. Kublai Khan, Emperor of the Yuan Dynasty, granted Pagba, the fifth founder, the title of Imperial Tutor. Later, Pagba was granted the title of Prince of Great Treasure to command thirteen 10, 000-households, pioneering the system of mixed temporal and religious

<< *Jokhang Monastery in Lhasa built during the period of songtsan Gambo.* CHEN ZONGLIE

· · · · · · · · · · · >>
Portraits of three generations of Tibetan Kinge--Songtsan Gambo (middle), Trisung Detsan (left) and Rabejun (Tashilhungpo Monastery mural).   CHEN ZONGLIE

administration.

The Gagyu Sect emphasized oral instruction and paid more attention to secret cultivation that depends on it (and from which the name is derived). This sect was founded in the 11th century. It had many branches and had two reincarnation systems from the very beginning, namely Shangba Gagyu and Dabu Gagyu. Shangba Gagyu flourished for a while. The Sengding Monastery was established by the sect, headed by a female Living Buddha holding a very high Buddhist position. Tongdong Gyibo, who was famous for building an iron bridge in the 15th century, was also a monk of Shangba Gagyu. But this sect disappeared in the 15th century. Dabu Gagyu continues to this day and its founder, Dabo Lhagyia Soinam Renqen, was born in Lhunzi County, Tibet. He studied medicine early in life and became monk at the age of 26. He majored in both the open and secret schools of Tibetan Buddhism and formally acknowledged Milha Riba as his teacher. Gradually the Dabo Gagyu Sect came into being. His four most famous disciples established monasteries and accepted disciples in the Lhasa area to form four major branches: Garma Gagyu, Chaba Gagyu, Barong Gagyu and Pagzhub Gagyu. In addition, Pagzhub Gagyu had eight sub-branches. The Garma Gagyu Sect was divided into the Black and Red Hat sects based on the gift of this headwear from the Yuan emperor. Reincarnation of Living Buddha was founded by the Black Hat Gagyu Sect. According to *Blue Annals*, in 1283, Garma Baxie, master of Curpu Monastery in the mountains northwest of Lhasa, told his disciples when dying, "I am going to leave for a while. After my death, the inheritor of the secret school of the Black Hat Sect will appear in Lhadui far away. Before his coming, you will serve as a temporary representative for Buddha." Then, he took off his gilt-edged hat and placed it on the head of Wogyiaba before dying.

In 1284, in Gungtang in the Xigaze area, the hometown of Milha Riba, master instructor of Gagyu Sect, a child was born. Five years later, he was recognized as the reincarnated soul boy of Garma Baxie. He was the first boy to be recognized as a reincarnated soul boy of a former monk in the history of Tibetan Buddhism. In 1289, this boy was invited to Curpu Monastery and became a monk following Wogyiaba, disciple of Garma Baxie. He was given the Buddhist name as Shangqoin Dorje. The details of this event were described in *Blue Annals*: When Shangqoin Dorje came to Curpu Monastery with his parents, he felt free to sit on the high seat facing Wogyiaba. Wogyiaba was astonished and asked, "Boy, why do you sit on my master's seat" Shangqoin Dorje answered, "Your master is me.î Wogyiaba suddenly recalled his master's last words and acknowledged that this boy was the reincarnation of his master. So, he said, iNow, take a seat below," and began to teach him.

The establishment of the Living Buddha Reincarnation System is the Garma Gagyu Sectís major contribution to Tibetan Buddhism. Before its establishment, there were mainly two modes of reincarnation among the religious sects. One was reincarnation from father to son or between fam-

<< . . . .
Samye Monastery in Zhaxiang county (built in the 8th century).
CHEN ZONGLIE

Tashilhungpo Monastery.   CHEN ZONGLIE

ily members; the other was reincarnation from master to disciple. The Nyingma Sect adopted the father-son mode. As the monks of this religious sect could marry and have children, a son could inherit the father's ëbusinessí. The significant representatives of the Nyingma Sect were a grandparent, a parent and a grandchild of three successive generations. Mingzhuling Monastery and Dorjezha Monastery, located respectively on the southern and northern banks of the Yarlung Zangbo River in the Lhasa area, were ancestral monasteries of the Nyingma Sect. In the middle period between 16th century and 17th century, these two monasteries adopted respectively incarnation from father to son and from father-in-law to son-in-law. Even today, Mingzhuling Monastery has a father-son incarnation system. In the Sagya Sect, family members inherited the dominant position. The first ancestral abbot of the Sagya Sect was Gunggar Nyingba, upon whose death his second son Soinam Zemo inherited the abbotship. When he died, his brother Zhaba Gyaincain became the third ancestral abbot, succeeded in due course by his nephew, who was Sagya Pandit Gungar Gyaincain, famous in history. After his death, his nephew Pagba inherited became the fifth ancestral master. Pagba acknowledged Kublai Khan, first Emperor of Yuan Dynasty, and was granted a title as Imperial Tutor, which made the Sagya Sect dominant in Tibet. However, the Gedan Sect adopted the mode of reincarnation from master to disciple. Its ancestral abbot Zongdainba had many disciples. He built up Razheng Monastery and asked his disciple Gungbawa to take over after his death, and this system remains today.

The Living Buddha Reincarnation System came into being in the 13th century and had its particular social historical background. At that time, Tibetan Buddhism was enjoying its second major propagation period. All religious sects built up their own monasteries and the independent monastic economy gradually came into being. Monasteries owned land, herds and pasture in addition to tenants. But this triggered severe political and economic competition and mutual mergers among the religious sects. In order to keep a stable position in the competition and to ensure they would continue to flourish, all the religious sects recognized that there must be an influential and steady leader, as well as a proper reincarnation system for passing on the post. Due to this

. . . . >>

Garma Bashie (tangka), leader of the
Black-Hat Garma Gagyu Sect.
　　　　　CHEN ZONGLIE

situation, different sects gradually adopted the Living Buddha Reincarnation System. Dorjezha Monastery of the Nyingma Sect, Sangding Monastery and Zhigung Monastery of the Gagyu Sect's Shangba Gagyu and others all changed their own former reincarnation mode to the Living Buddha Reincarnation system.

∨ *Lamas with the Zhaibung Monastery Performhg Buddhist rituals in Barkor Street, Lhasa.   CHEN ZONGLIE*

II. Gelug Sect Adopts the Living Buddha Reincarnation System

In the early days of the 15th century, the Gelug Sect flourished in Tibetan areas. Zongkapa Lobsang Zhaba (1357-1419) was its founder. He was born in the place where Qinghai Tar Monastery is located today. His father was a leader of Tibetan Longben Tribe and once served as an official of the Yuan Dynasty. At the age of seven, Zongkapa was sent by his family to Xaqoin Monastery by the Yellow River in what is now Hualong County, Qinghai Province. He became a monk following the eminent monk Toinzhub Renqen who returned from the U-Tsang area after learning Buddhism. At the age of 16 (1372), he went to Tibet to learn Buddhism. He formally acknowledged many famous scholars of religious sects as his teachers to learn the doctrines of the open and secret schools of Tibetan Buddhism. After the conclusion of his studies, he propagated Buddhist tenets and wrote books for preaching. With growing influence, he drew around him a group of disciples. In 1401, Zongkapa and his teacher Rendawa Xunnu Lozui (an eminent monk of Sagya Sect), as well as Gyiaqiao Besang (another eminent monk of the same sect who once received Rendawa and Zongkapa in Dagcangzong in 1390) called in hundreds of monks and held a Buddhist summons ceremony in Razheng Monastery, the ancestral monastery of the Gedan Sect. He called for the consolidation of religious discipline and the reformation of Tibetan Buddhism. This movement lasted for almost two years. But, towards the end, Rendawa and Gyiaqiao Besang left in quick succession, and after this. Zongkapa prepared to found his own sect instead of staying within the existing structure of the Sagya and Gagyu sects. From 1403 to 1419, when he died, a group of promising youths coming from various parts of Tibet assembled around Master Zongkapa. They became the skeleton force to establish the Gelug Sect. The important Living Buddha Reincar-

<< . . . . : . .
Gendun zhuba (1391-1474), a disciple of Zongkapa, later became the 1st Dalai Lama. The sculpture is preserved in the Tashilhungop Monastery.

CHEN ZONGLIE

nation System of the early Gelug Sect descends from one of these disciples, as does the Dalai Lama Living Buddha Reincarnation System.

In 1409, with the support from Dixi, the local political power in the Pagzhub area of Tibet holding the title of Prince of Propagation Zhaba Gyaincain granted by the Ming Dynasty, Zongkapa held the first Grand Summons Ceremony in Lhasa (at Jokhang Monastery) during the first Tibetan month. In the same year, he built up Gandain Monastery, the first to be established by the Gelug Sect, in Dagze County in northeastern Lhasa. Hence, a new sect of Tibetan Buddhism came into being. After its establishment, monks were sent to the Xigaze, Kham and Amdo areas to build respectively the Zhaibung Monastery, Sera Monastery, Tashilhungpo Monastery and others to further enhance its influence. Some monasteries of other religious sects (especially the numerous monasteries of Gedan Sect) submitted to or changed to the

Gelug Sect, enabling it to have monasteries all over Tibet and gradually grasp power. Emperor Yongle of the Ming Dynasty once invited Zongkapa to Beijing, but due to illness and too much business, he sent his disciple Shvakya-ye-shes in his place. Emperor Yongle granted him the title of Western Paradise Buddhist Grand National Master. Later, Emperor Xuande granted him as the title as Daxi Buddhist Master. The political and economic support from the court and the Prince of Propagation played an important role in the formation and early development of the Gelug Sect.

Early on, the Gelug Sect adopted the mode of inheritance from master to disciple. As Zongkapa took the post of abbot in Gandain Monastery, all the following abbots were recognized as the inheritor of Zongkapa's position. The supreme leader of religious sects was every abbot (that is Triba, pronounced as khri-pa in Tibetan) of Gandain Monastery, who is

Zongka (1357-1419) and his two disciples-Gyacaogyi (left) and Kezhubgyia (later the lst Panchen Erdeni) (right).
CHEN ZONGLIE

<< *Gandain Monastery.*　CHEN ZONGLIE

called Gandain Triba in Tibetan. As Zongkapa was viewed as an incarnation of the Wisdom Buddha, seven Gandain Tribas, including Gyiacaogyi and Kezhubgyia, after him were all born in the Xigaze area. Gandain Triba adopted the term system. Two masters of Tantri Zhacang (Lhasa Upper and Lower Tantric School) of Gandain Monastery served as Gandain Triba in turns. The inheritance system of Gandain Triba ensured the Gelug Sect's affairs were managed by an eminent monk, which played an important role in prevention of an internal power and maintenance of religious unity of the sect in this early period. Later, such a struggle did develop among the religious sects, because the monks who served as Gandain Triba were old and lacked energy. In addition, they were changed frequently without religious holiness and mystery, so they could not establish steady and long-term power in religion and politics. The designation system of Gandain Triba exposed its weakness. In order to strengthen its cohesive power and cultivate its own powerful leader, the Gelug Sect gradually adopted the Living Buddha Reincarnation system at the same time as maintaining the designation system of Gandain Triba. Thus, the religious theories and rules about Living Buddha Reincarnation came into being.

Living Buddha Reincarnation System is based mainly on incarnation theories. This theology is very popular and well known by disciples. They can accept the mode of Living Buddha Reincarnation without problems.

Simply speaking, the Living Buddha is Buddha or Bodhisattva who is living on earth in human form. After death, the Living Buddha can be born on earth once again, which is called reincarnation. After the repeated birth of the Living Buddha, he can be found out only after extensive searching. With the conclusion of searching and confirmation, he is called the "incarnated soul boy" before the holding of a sitting-in-the-bed ceremony to confirm him. After this, he can be called a Living Buddha soul boy. When a soul boys of a grand Living Buddha becomes adult, the central government granted him the title of Hotogtu. During childhood, the Living Buddha would undergo careful cultivation and strict religious education from monasteries. Once becoming an adult, he could inherit the position and political and economic power from the late religious leader.

After the Gelug Sect adopted Living Buddha Reincarnation System, many types of this mode of power transference appeared among the religious sects. The Dalai Lama Living Buddha Reincarnation System was formed earliest, spread by Gendun Zhuba, a disciple of Zongkapa in his

later years. Gendun Zhuba was the founder of Tashilhungpo Monastery, which was the largest of the Gelug Sect monasteries in the Xigaze area. The 2nd Dalai Lama Gendun Gyamco lived in Tashilhungpo Monastery in his early days, but later went to Lhasa Zhaibung Monastery and Sera Monastery. Because the largest Living Buddha Reincarnation System came into being within the Gelug Sect, it was natural for the Dalai Lama to become the supreme religious and political leader in the Gelug Sect.

∧ Statue of Gendun Gyamco (1475-1542) preserved in the Potala Palace: He was confirmed as the reincarnated soul boy of Gendun Zhuba at three, and was later enthroned as the 2nd Dalai Lama. CHEN ZONGLIE

15

III. The Title of the Dalai Lama Related to Gendun Zhuba and Gendun Gyamco

Gendun Zhuba and Gendun Gyamco were posthumously named the first and second holders of the title of Dalai Lama, and were the founders of Dalai Lama Living Buddha reincarnation system. But when they were alive, the word of "Dalai Lama" had not emerged and they could not imagine that they would have anything to do with a system that would play an important role in Tibetan history. Moreover, their Living Buddha reincarnation was only confirmed after a complex series of steps.

The title of the Dalai Lama first appeared in 1578. At that time, the Gelug Sect's grand Living Buddha Soinam Gyamco went to Mongolia to spread Buddhist doctrines at the invitation of the Tumet Mongol Prince of Shunyi Anta Khan. In Yinghua Monastery in Qinghai, he offered a comprehensive explanation of Tibetan Buddhism, which was praised by the Mongol Prince, who granted him the title of Dalai Lama. ìDalaiî means sea in Mongol language and ìLamaî means master in Tibetan. This is the origin of the title of Dalai Lama.

In this passage, the origin of the title of Panchen Living Buddha will also be introduced. As the two major reincarnation systems of Living Buddha of the Gelug Sect, the Dalai and Panchen have a close relationship in the development of Tibetan Buddhism and the Living Buddha Reincarnation System. The title of Panchen first appeared in 1645. At that time, after overthrowing the Dixi Tsangpa regime, the Khan of the Mongol and Shuote tribes granted Abbot Lobsang Qoigyi Gyaincain (1567-1622) of Tashilhungpo Monastery the title of "Panchen Poktog", following the example set by Anta Khan in granting Soinam Gyamco the title of Dalai Lama. Panchen means grand scholar. Thus, the Panchen

<< . . . .
Statue of the 3ʳᵈ Dalai Lama Soinam Gyamco (1543-1588) preserved in the Potala Palace. CHEN ZONGLIE

reincarnation Living Buddha system was established. According to tradition, Zongkapa's disciple Kezhugyi (1385-1438) was admitted posthumously as the first Panchen. His reincarnation, Soinam Qoinam (1439-1504), was the second Panchen, and Lobsang Toinzhub (1505-1566) became the third.

Since the title of Dalai Lama emerged from the third Dalai Lama, Soinam Gyamco, why were Gendun Zhuba and Gendun Gyamco admitted as his two immediate predecessors? It was because Soinam Gyamco was the reincarnation of Gendun Zhuba and Gendun Gyamco.

According to *Biography of the First Dalai Lama* written by Yexei Zemo (the fourth abbot of the Tashilhungpo Monastery), the first Dalai Lama Gendun Zhuba (1391-1474) was a resident of Srad in the Shabchu River drainage area in Sagya County of the Xigaze area. He came from a herding family. On the night he was born, robbers were pillaging the area. When his parents ran away, they hid him in a thick growth of grass, an experience he fortunately survived. When he was young, his family was very poor with no herds or land of their own. From the age of five, he had to help others graze sheep in order to support his family. At the age of seven, his father died. His mother went with her five sons and daughters to his uncle, Qoigyi Xerab, in the Natang Monastery to seek shelter and then worked for others in the nearby village for a pittance. Hence, the young boy often went to Natang Monastery to beg. He was very bright and a devout Buddhist. He went to the monastery dressed in the monk's clothes made by himself and attracted the attention of Abbot Zhuba Xerab. The abbot tonsured him and helped him to learn Buddhist doctrines, Sanskrit and Tibetan. Later, the young man followed Zongkapa's disciple, Shes-rab-seng-ge, who was famous for his preaching of Tantric doctrine and was the founder of the earliest Tantric Zhacang of the Gelug Sect as well as a fellow towns-man of Gendun Zhuba, living south of the mountain in the Lhasa area. He also followed Zongkapa, who sent him to Razheng Monastery to learn the religious disciplines. As a result, he was not present when Zongkapa died. After the latter's death, the boy acknowledged Shes-rab-seng-ge as his Buddhist teacher and returned with him to the Xigaze area. He began to teach his own disciples and spread Buddhist doctrines, gradually gaining fame. In 1447, he left Natang Monastery and built up Tashilhungpo Monastery with the support of local leaders, serving as its abbot. After more

∧ Ivory seal bearing text reading Dorchichang (meaning Diamond Club in Tibetan), a title Ming Dynasty Emperor Shengzong granted to Soinam Gyamco. It is preserved in the Norbu Lingka.
CHEN ZONGLIE

than 20 years of operation, Tashilhungpo Monastery became the major monastery of the Gelug Sect in the Xigaze area. Gendun Zhuba therefore became an important leader of the sect and was even recognized as the incarnation of the Goddess of Mercy by some devout disciples.

In his later years, Gendun Zhuba began to consider the issue of who should inherit his position. At that time, the Gelug Sect had not yet widely adopted the Living Buddha reincarnation system. So, he wanted to choose his successor from among his disciples, including Natangba Sangbo Zhaxi, Shangba Qenbo and some others, whom he hoped would each take the position in turn. After Gendun Zhuba died on December 8, 1474, Shangba Qenbo was asked to inherit his position. However, he insisted on divination and the casting of lots to determine the issue. The result showed that it was not proper for him to succeed at that time. Again asked to accept the post, he sought a second divination, which showed that Sangbo Zhaxi was fit to become abbot of Tashilhungpo Monastery. However, according to Gunggai Gyaincainís *The 12th Achievement of the first Dalai Lama Gendun Zhuba,* Gendun Zhuba handed his keys to his sermon masters in the monastery before his death. When asked how to handle the succession, he nominated Shangba Qenbo and the sermon masters take the post one after another. But, as already noted, Shangba Qenbo declined and, one month later, in favor of Sangbo Zhaxi. Thus, Gendun Zhuba did not have any plan about his ireincarnationî.

According to the autobiography of the second Dalai Lama, as well as *Biography of the Second Dalai Lama* written by Yang-guan-qu-jie, after the death of Gendun Zhuba, although Tashilhungpo Monastery adopted the reincarnation system from master to disciple, some disciples still believed that Gendun Zhuba would be reincarnated since the Living Buddha reincarnation mode had begun to gain popularity at that time. At first, Toinyuba, a lama of Tanapu, told the sermon masters of Tashilhungpo Monastery that, ìthere is a saying that Gendun Zhuba would be reincarnated in the Han area, but Buddhism there is not flourishing. I think he would not be reincarnated there. In case of reincarnation, the place of his reincarnation must be nearby, which is not within our knowledge. So the attendants and sermon masters should not blunder.î However, according to *Biography of the second Dalai Lama,* Tanapu is the hometown of the 2nd Dalai Lama, whose grandfather was Toinyu Gyaincain. He was a monk versed in the doctrines of all the sects and had a close relationship with old Gendun Zhuba. So, he must be this lama, Toinyuba. Gunggar Gyaincain was the father of the second Dalai Lama and studied at home the doctrines of the Gagyu and Gelug sects and once followed Bodong Banqen to study the sutras. His mother was named Gunggar Bemo, who also studied the ideas of the Gelug Sect. In infancy, the 2nd Dalai Lama Gendun Gyamco (1475-1542) was said to be very clever, showing many extraordinary traits of character. So, his families and the monks at Tanapu believed that he was the reincarnation of Gendun Zhuba. When he was 10, Tashilhungpo Monastery sent the attendants of Gendun Zhuba including Sengboin Zholma to invite him to the monastery. On June 4, 1486, Abbot Lungri Gyamco tonsured him and named him as Gendun Gyamco. Lungri Gyamco might have cultivated him as the reincarnation of Gendun Zhuba to eventually become the abbot of Tashilhungpo. But at the end of that year, the former resigned and was succeeded in 1487 by Yexei Zemo. This Yexei Zemo was the major master of Gendun Gyamco. But when he wrote the *Biography of the First Dalai Lama* in 1494, it did not mention that Gendun Gyamco was the reincarnation of Gendun Zhuba. So, it can be seen that, at that time, many masters in charge in Tashilhungpo Monastery did not acknowledge the identification of Gendun Gyamco as a reincarnated Living Buddha. Later, he studied Buddhism in Tashilhungpo Monastery, gradually becoming well known. It was said that, in November 1492, when he was 17 years old, monks from Tashilhungpo Monastery went to Gyangtze Nening Monastery in present-day Kangmo County to hold a summons ceremony, and the people who begged for a lucky blessing from him exceeded those for Abbot Yexei Zemo, and that this aroused jealousy among the latterís attendants. Moreover, Gendun Gyamco only offered food on one occasion for those monks studying Buddhism, so the attendants felt even more dissatisfied. The Natang Monastery Kampus Xerab Gyaincain said: "That person (referring to Gunggar Gyaincain, father of Gendun Gyamco) did not hold my master in reverence, so his son could not be the intellectual reincarnation of Gendun Zhuba." In view of the difficulties caused by these intrigues, Qoigyi Moinlangbei, a monk of Zhaibung Monastery, invited Gendun Gyamco to the Lhasa area, a journey the young man completed in February 1494. According to Gendun Gyamco himself, he asked for an interview with Yexei Zemo before his departure to eliminate conflict between master and disciple. But the request was rejected. When he arrived in Lhasa, he was welcomed by Zhaibung Monasteryís Abbot Gyangyang Leba Qunjor. This showed the difference in attitude between the two grand monasteries of the Gelug Sect over the issue of whether Gendun Gyamco was the reincarnation of Gendun Zhuba. After Gendun Gyamco joined Zhaibung Monastery, he followed Gyangyang Leba Qunjor to study the doctrines of the open and secret schools of Tibetan Buddhism. In 1495, he acknowledged formally Gyangyang Leba Qunjor and others as his teachers and received the bhiksu disciplines.

When Gendun Gyamco arrived in Lhasa, the Gelug Sect was in great difficulties. In 1481, the Renbangba family, followers of the Gagyu Sect who controlled local political power in Tibet, supported the Garma Gagyu Sect to build up two new monasteries in the eastern suburbs of Lhasa to repel the influence of the Gelug Sect in the city. They even took the demesne of Zhaibung Monastery and Sera Monastery near Lhasa by force and compelled some small Gelug Sect's monasteries to submit to the Gagyu Sect. From 1498, Renbangba even gave orders forbidding Gelug Sect monks to participate in the Lhasa Grand Summons Ceremony founded and held by Gelug Sect every year. Instead, they asked the Gagyu and Sagya sect's monks to stage the ceremony. Obviously, Renbangba aimed to push the Gelug Sect out of its originating place and chief base so as to weaken its power. So, the Gelug Sect faced a critical time. In this situation, its monks and common disciples felt they urgently needed a powerful leader who could lead them out of their difficulties. So, Gendun Gyamco, who was identified as a reincarnated Living Buddha (although this identification was not acknowledged by all in or outside of the religious sects) caught everyone's attention. In 1501, Gendun Gyamco went to Qoikegyi in Sangri County to spread Buddhism at the invitation of the local monastery and common leaders of the Gelug Sect in the Oika area. Later, he studied and preached all over the Lhasa area and established a relationship with monastery and common leaders everywhere. He gradually became a well-known eminent monk of the Gelug Sect. In 1509, he built up Qoikegyi Monastery in Oika subsidized by local monastery and common leaders. A year later, he was invited back by Tashilhungpo Monastery Abbot Yexei Zemo and other monks and returned to his home monastery. The conflict between him and his master Yexei Zemo was ended. In 1512, he succeeded Yexei Zemo as abbot. This also showed that, after over 30 years of competition and selection, the reincarnation link from master to disciple was finally accepted by everyone within

Tashilhungpo Monastery.
ZHU QILIANG

Tashilhungpo Monastery. Hence, the identification of Gendun Gyamco as the reincarnation of Gendun Zhuba was confirmed.

But Gendun Gyamco did not serve as Tashilhungpo Monastery's abbot cluring his life time like Gendun Zhuba. Instead, he could move on to become the leader of the whole Gelug Sect. In 1517, Gendun Gyamco was invited to take the post of Zhaibung Monastery's abbot. Supported by Pagzhub, he held the Lhasa Grand Summons Ceremony in the first Tibetan lunar month in 1518. The rights of Gelug Sect's monks to participate in the ceremony at this time was restored after 20 years of discontinuity, which played an important role in leading the sect out of its difficulties. In 1526, he took the post of Sera Monastery's abbot at the same time at the invitation of Sera Monastery's monks and became an eminent figure in the Gelug Sect with the higher position than Gandain Triba. Thus, after Gendun Gyamco died in 1542, it became natural to find his reincarnation. In accordance with the procedure that Gendun Gyamco was acknowledged as Gendun Zhuba's reincarnation, there was some difference and even conflict about whether reincarnation system would be adopted, but the temporal authorities did not intervene because it was a religious matter. Later, with the development of religious sects and monasteries, the eminent monks in power found it better to acknowledge a very young soul boy as the reincarnation of their master. In addition, the soul boy would not affect their own position and fame because of the great age difference, so they were more willing to accept the mode of Living Buddha reincarnation. Later, the conflict about the inheritance of religious leaders was not related to whether Living Buddha reincarnation would be adopted, but who would handle the search for and confirmation of the incarnated soul boy and the birthplace and family background of the soul boy. As it was related to the political and economic interests of monasteries, local region and families, common political powers soon began to participate in it.

With the promotion of the religious position of Gendun Gyamco in the Gelug Sect, his relationship with local power became closer. In 1518, Ngawang Zhaxi Zhaba, leader of the Pagzhub power group, who was granted the title as Prince of Propagation by the Ming Dynasty, presented his villa close to Zhaibung Monastery to Gendun Gyamco. This villa's name was changed to "Gandain Phodrang Palace" when the 3rd Dalai Lama Soinam Gyamco lived there. This name later became the name of the local government of the Gelug Sect in Tibet. This villa provided him not only with special house, but also with lands and residents belonging to his Living Buddha reincarnation system in addition to his own attendant group. This might be recognized as an embryonic form of Lhadrang organization of the grand Living Buddha of the Gelug Sect. Thus, Gendun Gyamco became a true Living Buddha in terms of modern religious and social meaning.

IV. The Development of the Reincarnation of the Dalai Lama: Soinam Gyamco and Yundain Gyamco

According to the record in *Biography of the 3ʳᵈ Dalai Lama* by the 5ᵗʰ Dalai Lama, immediately after Gendun Gyamco's demise in the third Tibetan month of 1542, many people discussed the issue of his soul boy, turning to the answers and auguries from eminent monks by inviting deities to descend.

In the 11ᵗʰ Tibetan month of 1542, Soinam Gyamco was born to an aristocratic family at Kangsagung in Doilungdeqen County. Stories about his intelligent actions became popular within the family and among local monks and lay people. It was written in the *Biography of the 3ʳᵈ Dalai Lama* that there was a close connection between the actions of the parents and the dreams of the eminent monks. These legends soon came to the attention of the abbot from Zhaibung Monastery, Benqen Soinam Zhaba (author of the famous Tibetan historical work *New Red Annals)* and some local headmen. In 1545, Benqen Soinam Zhaba interviewed 3-year-old Soinam Gyamco at a Buddhist conference held at Jormolung Monastery (located in Doilungdeqen County and not far from where the boy was born) to test his intellectual powers. It was said that Soinam Zhaba brought out a painting of the master's image and asked the boy if he could recognize it. The boy replied that it was he who had given the painting to Soinam Zhaba, which made the latter believe the youngster certainly was the soul boy of Gendun Gyamco. Later, Gendun Gyamco's attendant Zongnan Renboche and his retinue were sent by Zhaibung Monastery to Kangsagung to test the boy. They asked him to identify the image of Tara and Subhah that were carried by Gendun Gyamco when he was alive. Benqen Soinam Zhaba and Zongnan Renboche eventually affirmed the child as the soul boy of Gendun Gyamco. Neqoin from Zhaibung Monastery also presented his opinion during the process. After consultation between Zongnan Renboche and the

abbot of Zhaibung Monastery, (who had been given the title of Prince of Propagation by the Ming Dynasty), the soul boy was invited to the Zhaibung Monastery in March 1547 with the approval of Disi of the Pagmo Zhuba regime (equivalent to the Prince of Propagation). Upon arrival at Zhaibung Monastery, Soinam Gyamco was welcomed by all the monks and laymen. Two seats were placed in Gendun Gyamcoís residence Gandain Phodrang Palace with Abbot Soinam Zhaba and Soinam Gyamco sitting abreast. The headman of Pagmo Zhuba, all the monks, lay people and benefactors of the monastery offered their presents to the soul boy. An upasaka (layman) ceremony was held for Soinam Zhaba to be his teacher, and for him to be given the religious name of Soinam Gyamco. It was the first time that a soul boy as the Living Buddha Dalai Lama had been located, confirmed and conferred in the sitting-in-the-bed ceremony. It was also the first time for Neqoin from Zhaibung Monastery to be involved. But all the activities were initiated by Zhaibung Monastery and presided over by the Abbot Benqen Soinam Zhaba of Zhaibung Monastery in line with the willingness of himself, the monks and the laymen. Although the headman of Pagmo Zhuba had been consulted and he attended the sitting-in-the-bed ceremony of Soinam Gyamco and gave his instruction, it was not plausible to conclude that it was the headman of Pagmo Zhuba who sanctified the affirmation of the soul boy. Therefore, the inspection,confirmation and sitting-in-the-bed ceremony of the 3rd Dalai Lama were no different from those of the soul boy of the Living Buddha of other religious sects. Consequently, Soinam Gyamco was called the soul boy of the living Buddha of the Zhaibung Monastery.

In 1552, with the management of Benqen Soinam Zhaba, 10-year-old Soinam Gyamco assumed the abbot of Zhaibung Monastery as the inheritor of Benqen Soinam Zhaba, and presided over the Grand Summons Ceremony in 1553. Actually, Benqen Soinam Zhaba set several precedents in regard to the affairs of the soul boy as the Living Buddha of Dalai Lama. First, the disciple who had been acting as the abbot of Zhaibung Monastery during the last Dalai Lama's presidency took on the presiding work, initiated the *upasaka* (layman) ceremony for the soul boy and was in charge of the soul boy's education; secondly, during the process of confirmation, the leaders of the local government of Tibet had been consulted; thirdly, the new Dalai Lama soon took the position as the Zhaibung Monastery abbot; fourthly, Soinam Gyamco was assisted to preside over the Grand Summons Ceremony when he was only 11. These measurements demonstrated the exigent wishes of the Gelug Sect leadership to prop up Soinam Gyamco as their new head. After Soinam Gyamco, the abbotship of Zhaibung Monastery was assumed by nobody else but the Dalai Lama with the exception of a period of time when the 4th Panchen Erdeni took over the office after the 4th Dalai Lamaís demise due to the ban on seeking a soul boy for Dalai Lama by the Disi Tsangba Sect regime. The subsequent abbot of Sera Monastery followed the same procedure. Thus, the leadership of Dalai Lama of Gelug Sect was solidified in that only the Dalai Lama could take up the position as abbot of both Zhaibung Monastery and Sera Monastery. After Benqen Soinam Zhaba's demise, the Gelug Sect also started to look for his soul boy, and a soul boy system was established in Zhaibung Monastery in an effort to memorize his feats for the Dalai Lama and the achievements he acquired as the 15th Gandain Chiba Abbot, and the Zhaibung and Sera Monastery abbot. Such a form of award greatly prompted the enthusiasm of many eminent monks of the Gelug

Sect seeking and confirming soul boys for their masters, and promoted the establishment of the soul boy system of the living Buddha in the Gelug Sect.

The efforts of the eminent monks of Gelug Sect in enhancing the leadership of Soinam Gyamco to build up their authority helped intensify the sectís solidarity and stability. In addition, the period of the rise of the Disi Tsangba family, and their defeat of Renbengba in the years after 1557, had a cushioning effect for the Gelug Sect in regard to its external environment. Taking advantage of this, Soinam Gyamco traveled to several places in the Xigaze area, setting up relations with the local headmen to expand the influence of the Gelug Sect, and even spread knowledge of the section among the Mongolian nationality.

In 1576, when Althan Khan, the headman of the Mongol Tumet tribe was migrating with his followers to Qinghai Province, he invited Soinam Gyamco to Qinghai for an interview, which marked a turning point for the status of both the Gelug Sect and Soinam Gyamco himself. Despite the opposition from some sect members, Soinam Gyamco resolutely accepted the invitation and started out from Lhasa in 1577. In the summer of 1578, he met Althan Khan at Chabochiyale—a place beside Qinghai Lake, and managed to convert several Mongolian leaders to the Gelug Sect. As a demonstration of Althan Khan's admiration for Soinam Gyamco's profound Buddhist knowledge, he endowed the title "Dalai Lama". Hence, the title had been brought into the soul boy system, and became the symbol of the Living Buddha worshiped by the headmen in all the Mongolian tribes. Because Soinam Gyamco became the leader of Gelug Sect as the soul boy of Gendun Gyamco, and Gendun Gyamco built up his position in the Gelug Sect as the soul boy of Gendun Zhuba, Soinam was confirmed as the 3rd Dalai Lama by the upper leadership of the Gelug Sect, with Gendun Gyamco as the second and Gendun Zhuba, the disciple of old Zongkapa and the builder of Tashilhungpo Monastery, as the first.

<<*Lamas involved in heated debate on doctrines of Buddhism. WANG XINGGUANG*

Antagonism had long existed between Althan Khan and the Ming Dynasty. However, the two sides had become reconciled before Althan Khan arrived in Qinghai, and he was given the title of "Shunyi Prince" by the Ming Dynasty. Soinam Gyamco also established relations with the Ming Dynasty through Althan Khan, and interviewed some local Ming officials in Ganzhou on invitation.

On the basis of historical records, when Soinam Gyamco was in Ganzhou, he wrote a letter through Doutang (Governor of Gansu) to the Prime Minister Zhang Juzheng of the Ming Dynasty as follows, "How are you? I keep chanting Buddhist scriptures for the emperor and for the peace of our country. Here, I present my gifts for you including a statue of the Goddess of Mercy with four arms and pulu woolen fabrics. I will tell Shunyi Prince to return with your instructions. —Written in early December of 1578 or the Lunar Year of the Tiger". As Soinam Gyamco persuaded Althan Khan to return Tumet from control of Qinghai in accordance with the request of the Ming Dynasty, Soinam Gyamco won the honorific title of Dorchichang from the Ming court. What's more, upon his request, he had been permitted to pay tribute to the Ming Dynasty regularly as the leader of the Tibetan religion. After Soinam Gyamco's interview with Althan Khan, Gelug Sect monasteries had been constructed in Amdo and the Kham area, where Mongolian monks were tonsured. Thereafter, Gelug Sect doctrines spread to Chahar, Kurka and other tribes in Mongolia. Among the retinue of the 3rd Dalai Lama, there was one who assumed the office of the Sera Monastery abbot named Dongkel Yundain Gyamco and later became a prominent Living Buddha system with a soul boy in Mongolian activities. Some Mongolian aristocrats were affirmed as the soul boys of the eminent monks in the Gelug Sect, and in this way several soul boy systems were established in various Mongolian tribes to gain the support from all Mongolian military forces, strengthening and improving the status of the Gelug Sect and the Dalai Lama. With the great enhancement of Dalai Lamaís leadership in the Gelug Sect, new political factors imbued the subsequent soul boy affairs of the Dalai Lama.

In March 1588, the 3rd Dalai Lama Soinam Gyamco passed away in Inner Mongolia on his way to Beijing at the invitation of the Ming Dynasty. In 1589, the next year after his demise, the wife of Sumir Taiji, one of Althan Khan's grandsons (namely Banhan Zhulha, daughter of Nornorhe Weizhennoryan, 16th-generation grandson Nornorhe Weizhennoryan of Genghis Khan's brother Hashar), gave birth to a boy.

After the birth of this son, word spread quickly among the aristocrats in the Tumet tribe and the retinue of the 3rd Dalai Lama that the boy was the Dalai Lama Soinam Gyamco's soul boy. In October of the same year, Minister Gyamco wrote to the Gelug Sect, reporting the boyís birth and the intelligent things. At the time, sect leaders were in the process of inspecting a child in Zhigung to test whether he was the soul boy of the 3rd Dalai Lama, but abandon the task as soon as they received the letter. A delegation led by Minister Gyamco was dispatched to Inner Mongolia. Among its members were headman of Pagmo Zhuba and representatives of local aristocrats in Lhasa and the three major monasteries. Before departure, Banjor Gyamco had been relieved of his office as Gandain Chiba Abbot and the child had been named as Yundain Gyamco, which demonstrated that the soul boy born in Inner Mongolia had already been affirmed as the 4th Dalai Lama. As the delegation reached Mongolia, the soul boy had been invited to Hohhot and sanctified by the local monks and laymen. According to the reports in *Biography of the 4th Dalai Lama* by the 5th Dalai Lama, when the leader of Pagmo Zhuba got the news that the soul boy was to leave for Tibet, he wrote a eulogy blessing the soul boy and urging him to study hard, by which he demonstrated his recognition of the 4th Dalai Lama on behalf of the local government of Tibet (although Pagmo Zhuba was in imminent danger at the time). As the top authority of Gelug Sect, the soul boy was transferred to a Mongolian aristocrat's family, which marked a significant choice of the Gelug Sect and an essential development in soul boy system of the Dalai Lama.

When the 4th Dalai Lama arrived at Lhasa in 1603, he was welcomed by Lhasa monks and lay people. After he mounted the monastic seat of the 3rd Dalai Lama, he was tonsured and taught the Buddhist scripture in Jokhang Monastery by Gandain Chiba Abbot Sanggyi Renqen and Gandain Chiba Abbot Gendun Gyaincain who had been relieved of their offices for this purpose. As a result of some interior conflicts in the Gelug Sect, however, Sanggyi Renqen resigned and Gendun Gyaincain refused to act as his by citing his advanced age as the excuse. With the adoption of his proposal, Lobsang Qoigyi Gyaincain (1570-1662, the 4th Panchen), who was the Tashilhungpo Monastery abbot, was invited as the teacher of Yundain Gyamco. This was the first time that a master acted as the teacher of Dalai Lama. From then on, the soul boy of the Panchen stepped onto the central stage of Tibetan history, and gradually became another essential soul boy system second only to that of Dalai Lama.

In 1604, Yundai Gyamco and Lobsang Qoigyi Gyaincain headed for Qoikegyi Monastery to worship. In December 1614, the 4th Dalai Lama had Panchen Lobsang Qoigyi Gyaincain as his teacher, and he held bhiksu rituals for the former. An Upasaka (layman) ceremony was a matter of vital importance for a Buddhist monk. That Lobsang Qoigyi Gyaincain held the *bhiksu* ceremony for Yundai Gyamco indicated the precedent of mutual initiation of the *bhiksu* ceremony between the soul boy system of the Panchen Erdeni and the Dalai Lama. Although there was no definite regulation on the issue, the mutual initiation of *bhiksu* ceremony occurred periodically between the Dalai Lama and the Panchen, which turned out to be an important content in the relationship between the two sides.

With the indoctrination of Panchen Lobsang Qoigyi Gyaincain and the eminent monks of Gelug Sect, Yundain Gyamco soon managed to adapt his identity as Dalai Lama. He presided over the Grand Summons Ceremonyin Lhasa in 1604. Yundain Gyamco brought Mongolian military forces with him when coming to Tibet, which provided significant assistance and support to the Gelug Sect. Though Disi Tsangba, who had taken over the Renbengba family's status, showed tougher suppression and greater hostility to the Gelug Sect than had Renbengba, The Gelug Sect kept on developing steadily under pressure with the support from the Mongolian armed forces, which simultaneously deepened the religious conflicts between the Gelug Sect and the Garma Gagyu Sect.

In 1616, the 4th Dalai Lama was bestowed with the title iMaster of Vajradharaî, along with an official seal, by Emperor Wanli of Ming Dynasty. According to the original record in *Biography of the 4th Dalai Lama,* "in the third month of the Tibetan Year of Fire Dragon or 1616, Ming Emperor Wanli accredited a group of Han people led by Soinam Lozui to grant the title, official seal, and vestment on Dalai Lama at Gyiagyikang (office of the Han) of Zhaibung Monastery."

Facing the monastery, the Dalai Lama prayed and scattered *qingke* barley in the air, at which time miracles emerged. The barley penetrated each corner inside and outside the monastery, and, more surprisingly, flowers sprang from the breasts of some statues of Buddha.

Before Yundain Gyamco's departure at the emperor's invitation, he unexpectedly passed away at the age of 28 in December 1616 at Zhaibung Monastery. It was said that the 4th Dalai Lama was murdered by someone sent by Tsangpa Khan Puncog Namgyi, who believed that it was the 4th Dalai Lamaís curse on him that resulted in his ultimately fatal disease. This story might be possible, but there was no certainty that the Dalai Lamaís death was due to this "curse", but possibly from the power struggle between the two feudal lords. Thus, it was clear that Dalai Lama had been at the center of political conflicts in Tibet as early as the 4th Dalai Lamaís period, and the fate of Dalai Lama was at the core of those conflicts.

V . The Confirmation of the 5ᵗʰ Dalai Lama

Not long after the 4ᵗʰ Dalai Lama's demise, in 1618, the local aristo-crat Gyixoipa, who supported Gelug Sect, allied with Mongol troops to fight Disi Tsangba in Lhasa; the former gained the upper hand at first, but was ultimately defeated. With victory, Disi Tsangba gave orders to expropriate the manors and subjects of the aristocrats from Zhaibung Monastery and Lhasa to penalize the Gelug Sect. He also prohibited the process of looking for the soul boy of the 4ᵗʰ Dalai Lama Yundain Gyamco with the ultimate purpose of cancel-ing the soul boy system of Dalai Lama. This, in turn, would result in a sense of frustration among the monks and lay people of the Gelug Sect, who would face difficulty in raising a new powerful leader among them. This was an important issue in the Tibetan history of a local force interfering in the Dalai Lama soul boy affairs.

In September of the same year, Ngawang Lobsang, who was later confirmed as the 5ᵗʰ Dalai Lama, was born at Qoingyi. His father Dudu Rabtan was born into the Qoingyi Hor family, which had a close rela-tionship with the Pagmo Zhuba regime. But he had friendly ties with Disi Tsangba, and it was through the arrangement of Disi Tsangbo Puncog Namgyi, that he married Gonggar

Statue of the the 5ᵗʰ Dalai Lama Lobsang Gyamco (1617-1682), preserved in the Potala Palace.
CHEN ZONGLIE

>> *Statue of Hoshod Mongol Chief Gushri Khan
preserved in the Potala Palace.   CHEN ZONGLIE*

Lhaze, the daughter of Nanggarze clan of the
Xigze area, in 1616.

In 1619, internal turmoil flared up in
Qoingyi. The mother and the son were endangered because Gonggar Lhaze
was regarded as the informer of Disi Tsangba at Qoingyi. With Disi
Tsangbaís approval, the mother and son rushed back to Nanggarze that
very night. Dudu Rabtan also left Qoingyi, but was placed under house
arrest at Xigaze by Disi Tsangba.

In July 1621, Tumet Mongol troops from Qinghai invited by Gelug
Sect defeated Disi Tsangba's troops in Lhasa. At the time, the 4th Panchen
acted as mediator in admonishing Mongol troops to cease the fight, and
enabled the Gelug Sect to resume their administrative power in Lhasa
and regain the manors and subjects of which they had been deprived of in
1618. It was at this time that Disi Tsangba Puncog Namgyi died of disease,
and his son Garma Dainjoin Wangbo succeeded to his post. With the
inter vention of Mongol troops, the ban onseeking soul boy for the 4th
Dalai Lama Yundain Gyamco had actually been imperceptibly annulled.

The leadership of Gelug Sect, the 4th Panchen and Gongqoi Qunpei,
who had held office as Gandan Chiba Abbot, immediately launched a
search to locate the soul boy for the 4th Dalai Lama. After the 4th Panchen
Erdeni and some other people selected one of the *three zanba* balls that
contained the name of the soul boy in front of the statue of the Wisdom
Buddha in the Razheng Monastery, Ngawang Lobsang Gyamco was chosen among the three candidates. This was the first time that the soul boy

of a living Buddha was selected by the deity. Later, the other two boys were confirmed as the soul boys of other living Buddhas, which demonstrated that there existed intense competition among several candidates This turned out to be a way for the solution of the problem.

After the confirmation of the soul boy of the 4th Dalai Lama, representatives from Zhaibung Monastery and Mongolia headed for Xigaze to report the confirmation of the soul boy to Disi Tsangba. Some people in the Disi Tsangba regime maintained that the soul boy should live and study at Tashilhungpo Monastery in Xigaze for better control, which was strongly opposed by the delegate of the Gelug Sect, who insisted on settling the soul boy in Zhaibung Monastery for the sitting-in-the-bed ceremony, taking the approach of Mongol troops to Xigaze area as the cause. Supporters of the Disi Tsangba regime found it hard to reach an agreement, and ultimately Disi Tsangba had to agree to invite the soul boy to Zhaibung Monastery for the sitting-in-the-bed ceremony, and to live there studying scriptures.

Escorted by representatives from Mongolia and the Gelug Sect in February 1622, Ngawang Lobsang started out from his uncle's house to Zhaibung Monastery. As a result of the fact that neither Ngawang Lobsang's parents or his uncle were disciples of the Gelug Sect, he could not be accompanied by any of them, which made for a lonely journey. His nurse returned to Nanggarze after living with him in Zhaibung Monastery for a short period. After a couple of years, the father of the 5th Dalai Lama passed away during his imprisonment, but the son could only hold the ceremony of releasing his father's soul from purgatory in secret. These facts explained that before Gelug Sect was in power, no relatives of Dalai Lama could benefit politically or economically as a result of the confirmation of the soul boy of Dalai Lama. Ngawang Lobsang Gyamco was welcomed by Qianzu Soinam Qunpei of the 4th Dalai Lama upon his arrival at Nyingtang. With the arrangement of some Mongolian and Tibetan people, the Zhaibung Monasteryís Gandain Phodrang held the sitting-in-the-bed ceremony and the soul boy became the 5th Dalai Lama.

After the ceremony, the Gelug Sect finally achieved tranquility and stability after 10 years of turmoil, with the support of Tumet tribe. The Ming Dynasty was in a precarious situation at that time. Manchuria was on the upsurge led by Norhachi and his son Huantaichi, who founded the Later Jin. Lingdan Khan from the Mongol Chahar won over Tumet, but was defeated by the Later Jin.

In 1632, Qoitu Khan from Korgas was expelled during a convulsion at Korgas, and headed southward to Qinghai, where he conquered the Tumet tribe. Qoitu Khan favored the Garma Gagyu Sect religiously. It was recorded that Qoitu Khan was a disciple of Han Taoism, and when he first arrived in Qinghai, he invited many eminent monks of the Gelug Sect, thus demonstrating his friendliness. Influenced by his political ally, Lingdan Khan from the Chahar tribe, he adopted a hostile attitude toward Gelug Sect, imprisoned and killed its monks in Qinghai.

∧∧ *Gandan Phodrang of the Zhaibung Monastery, which was the local regime established by the 5th Dalai Lama with support from Gushri Khang.*

CHEN ZONGLIE

Meanwhile, Baili Headman Toinyu Dorje from the Kham area occupied Dege and some other places in the Kham area. He was a disciple of the Bon religion who opposed Buddhism and attacked the monasteries of the Sagya Sect, Gelug Sect and Nyingma Sect, arresting and imprisoning monks. With the instigation of the Living Buddhas of the Red-Hat System of the Garma Gagyu Sect, an alliance comprising Disi Tsangba, Qoitu Khan and the Baili Headman was set up, aiming to smash the power of the Gelug Sect. Furthermore, Qoitu Khan associated with Lingdan Khan, who showed an inclination towards the Gelug Sect at first but later converted to the Garma Gagyu Sect, to form a more powerful political and military alliance to dominate Qinghai and Tibet. In 1634, Lingdan Khan led his army to Qinghai, but Dachaotan died of disease on the way, and Qoitu Khan's purpose of joining forces with Lingdan Khan failed.

In 1635, Qoitu Khan sent his son Alslan to lead 10,000 troops from Qinghai to Tibet to associate with Disi Tsangba and wipe out the Gelug Sect, throwing the latter into panic. Alslan, however, changed his father's plan into smashing Disi Tsangba before dealing with the Gelug Sect to establish his dominion in Tibet, thus providing the Gelug Sect with a breathing spell. Under such circumstances, Qianzu Soinam Qunpei of the 5ᵗʰ Dalai Lama from the Gelug Sect sent representatives to Xinjiang to invite the headman of the Mongol Welt tribes, who had just converted to the Gelug Sect, to dispatch relief forces. At the end of 1636, Gushri Khan, headman of the Hoshot tribe in Welt led his troops into Qinghai, helping the Gelug Sect to pull through the crisis.

When the 5ᵗʰ Dalai Lama was 26 years old in 1642, the Gelug Sect, allied with troops of Gushri Khan, wiped out Disi Tsangba and came into power. Tibet was ruled by the Gelug Sect and the Mongol Hoshot, with Gushri Khan wielding military power. The 5ᵗʰ Dalai Lama was honored as a religious chief, and the new Potala Palace was constructed from 1644 as his residence. What's more, the number of Dalai Lama's retinue institutions and his attendants increased. Thus, Dalai Lama became a special living Buddha beyond those of the other sects in Tibetan Buddhism. Also, Gushri Khan gave the title ïPanchen Bokdoî to the 4th Panchen, making him another significant leader in the Gelug Sect with Diba Soinam Qunpei, who was appointed by Gushri Khan, taking charge of administrative affairs. Gushri Khan and the 5th Dalai Lama awarded manors, land and serfs to monasteries, monks and lay people who had contributed to the Gelug Sect. Consequently, the feudal serf system that combined politics with religion was strengthened and developed, and so the social base for Gelug Sect to control the local government had been established as well.

After the foundation of the Qing Dynasty in 1644, Emperor Shunzhi invited the 5th Dalai Lama to Beijing, and received him there in 1652. When he was on his way back, at Daihai in Liangcheng County of Inner Mongolia, officials led by Minister of Rites Jorlhu Namchiu and Minister Xidali in Charge of Religious Affairs in Mongolia and Tibet were dispatched by the Qing Dynasty, taking golden sheets bearing texts in Manchurian, Tibetan and Han Chinese and the golden seal of author ity to Daihai to grant Dalai Lama the title of "Overseer of the Buddhist

<< · · · · · · · · · · ·

Mural in Western Hall of the Potala Palace, which recorded how the 5th Dalai Lama led some 5000 men to pay homage to Qing Emperor Shunzhi in Beijing in 1652.   CHEN ZONGLIE

Faith on Earth under the Great Benevolent Self-Subsisting Buddha of Western Paradise", together with the golden sheets, and the golden seal of authority. Dalai Lama started using the golden seal of authority immediately. It was recorded in *Biography of the 5th Dalai Lama* that at the time, the Qing Emperor awarded Dalai Lama the golden seal of authority and golden sheets which read 'Dalai Lama, Overseer of the Buddhist Faith on Earth under the Great Benevolent Self-Subsisting Buddha of Western Paradiseí in Han Chinese, Tibetan and Mongolian. The golden sheets were the thickest in symmetry and they were four fingers wide and one *Ka* long (length measured with thumb and middle finger, which are stretched in the shape of a triangle). Its 15 pages were connected together and could be folded.

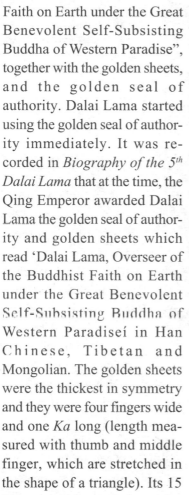

∧ *Huangsi Monastery the Qing emperor built in Beijing as residence of the visiting 5th Dalai Lama.*   CHEN ZONGLIE

∧ *Seal of authority the Qing emperor granted the 5th Dalai Lama for the exercise of leadership over Buddhism under the heaven.î From then on. All the Dalai Lama enjoyed the title. Here is the seal of authority for the 7th Dalai Lama.* CHEN ZONGLIE

The Tibetan on the golden seal of authority was translated by a Mongolian, thus it might seem somewhat unskilled. But the above were translated by an experienced Han translator.

<< *The 5th Dalai Lama ordered in 1645 to have the Potala Palace repaired. He moved from Gandain Phodrang of the Zhaibung Monastery to the Palace in 1653. Pictured here is a mural that records celebrations held to mark construction of the Palace.*
CHEN ZONGLIE

Meanwhile, Gushri Khan was conferred with the title of "Righteous and Wise Gushri Khan" by the Qing Emperor. Consequently, the Dalai Lama's position as religious leader in Tibet was set up with conferment by the central court. After Pagba from the Sagya Sect won the title of ìImperial Tutor from the Yuan Dynasty and Deying Xieba gained the title of Great Treasure Prince of Dharma by the Ming Dynasty, the successive Dalai Lamas of Gelug Sect were confirmed in their religious leadership by the Qing Emperor.

When the 5th Dalai Lama went to pay homage to the emperor in Beijing, the Qing Dynasty and remnants of the Southern Ming were still at war, which made the journey a dreadful one. Furthermore, massive struggles against Qing Dynasty broke out in succession around 1648 in places such as Gansu and Datong along the inevitable route for the 5th Dalai Lama. Even when he reached Beijing, struggles were still going on at Wutaishan Mountain, making it difficult for him to pay homage there as Pagba and Deying Xieba had done. However, he resolutely headed for Beijing with the purpose of strengthening the Gelug Sect's dominant position with the support of the central court.

However, before Gushri Khanís demise at the end of 1654 and Diba Soinam Qunpeiís demise in 1658, the 5th Dalai Lama merely possessed limited administrative power. Given Gushri Khan's strong hold on the Mongol troops, he had been relied on by the Gelug Sect to suppress revolts against its regime. Soinam Qunpei acted as Qianzu of the 4th Dalai Lama, assisted the 5th Dalai Lama, and played a vital role in the alliance between the Gelug Sect and Gushri Khan in seizing power in Tibet. In deciding affairs of great importance, they sometimes neglected the opinions of the 5th Dalai Lama, who had no alternative but to agree. Such records can be frequently read in the *Biography of the 5th Dalai Lama,* written by the Dalai Lama himself.

After Gushri Khan's demise, his children fought for power with the result that none of his children was able to take up the Khan position for three years running. The problem was solved through consultation. Of Gushri Khan's children, Dashibatur had been involved with the Qinghai Hoshot tribe while Dayankhan engaged in Tibetan political affairs until his succession in Lhasa in 1658.

Then Daba Soinam Qunpei passed away, and the 5th Dalai Lama was in a favorable position of being honored by the Qing Dynasty and was able to grant Khan titles to the leaders of the Hoshot tribe. With the support of the leadership of the Gelug Sect, the 5th Dalai Lama decisively seized the power of Diba appointments. The successive Dibas were all selected from among the trusted persons and attendants of the 5th Dalai Lama. Due to the incompetence of Dayankhan and his successors, political power in Tibet gradually shifted to the 5th Dalai Lama.

The 5th Dalai Lama escaped with his mother from their family in his early age, and later on, his father was imprisoned by Disi Tsangba in

Statue of the 5th Dalai Lama
preserved in the Potala Palace.
CHEN ZONTGLIE

Xigaze where he passed away. Therefore, the 5th Dalai Lama seldom contacted the Qoingyiba family of his father. He spent his childhood with his uncle, who belonged to the Nanggarze family and embraced the Jorxiang Sect that opposed the Gelug Sect. Religious factors resulted in his estrangement from his parents and his uncle, which in turn made him seek a way out spiritually among his trusted people in Lhasa and through developing an affinity with the Zongmaiba family in Lhasa.

Zongmaiba Chilai Gyamco, one of Dalai Lamaís attendants accompanying him to Beijing, was appointed Diba in 1660 after there had been a two-year vacancy. He then brought his nephew, 8-year-old Sanggyi Gyamco, to the Potala Palace and educated the boy himself.

After Zongmaiba Chilai Gyamco's death in 1668, one of the attendants of the 5th Dalai Lama was appointed to take over his post. Several years later, the 5th Dalai Lama became discontented about the affinity between Lobsang Tudao and the Naidong family in Shannan. In 1675, with the inducement of great amount of manors and serfs in Shannan, Lobsang Tudao abdicated his post as Diba.

At the time, the 5th Dalai Lama offered 23-year-old Sanggyi Gyamco the position of Diba, but the latter refused on the excuse of his young age. Instead, Qoiboin Abbot Lobsang Jinba, who was engaged in reli-

<< · · · · · · · · · · · · · · ·

The 5ᵗʰ Dalai Lama appointed Sanggyi Gyamco as Diba in his late years, and issued a document with his hand print to make public that the Diba would take over his power to rule Tibet. The document also told of the latter's knowledge and ability, asking all lamas and lay people to support him.
CHEN ZONTGLIE

gious activities for Living Buddha, was appointed, although agreeing to resign in three years. Upon his resignation in 1679, Sanggyi Gyamco took over his position. The 5ᵗʰ Dalai Lama specially issued a proclamation, introducing Sanggyi Gyamco's moral character, knowledge and capability to the monks and lay people, urging them to support him. He left his own fingerprints on the proclamation for confirmation. This writ was later included in *Selected Works by the 5ᵗʰ Dalai Lama,* and written completely in delicate strokes on the southern wall at the entrance of the Potala Palace with the fingerprints made of golden powder. The writ we can see now is not the original, but was one copied during the period of 13ᵗʰ Dalai Lama.

When the 5ᵗʰ Dalai Lama was alive, he requested Sanggyi Gyamco to wield the administrative power in Tibet under his supervision. After his demise, Sanggyi Gyamco could maintain his position and would be engaged in the confirmation and cultivation of the soul boy of the 5ᵗʰ Dalai Lama, to whom power would be transferred. In order to achieve his goal, he indicated to Sanggyi Gyamco before his death to hold a secret funeral and stealthily seek for the soul boy.

Thus, Sanggyi Gyamco withheld the news of the 5ᵗʰ Dalai Lama's demise for over 10 years, during which time he held power in Tibet in the name of the Dalai Lama, and was in charge of the confirmation of the soul boy. The intention in doing so was to avoid the interference from the Khan in Hoshot, not taking into account some historical factors. First, the relationship of political subordination to the central court had been set up in Tibet, while in tackling the significant affairs such as Dalai Lama's demise and the confirmation of soul boy, the central government of Qing Dynasty had been completely neglected. Conflicts between Sanggyi Gyamco and the central court would inevitably emerge with the enhancement of domination over the whole nation. That Sanggyi Gyamco showed sympathy and inclination to Gandain in the struggles against the Qing Dynasty at Zunggar Gandain incurred greater suspicion and antipathy on the part of Emperor Kangxi. Secondly, it was Hoshot tribe that had assisted the Dalai Lama in setting up his political power; thus, repulsing the headman of Hoshot would necessarily intensify the conflict and result in discord between the leadership of Mongolia and Tibet. Thirdly, such behavior was contrary to the routines in dealing with the soul boy affairs of the previous Dalai Lamas, during which time lay people were seldom involved in political power, but competition and conflict still emerged among monks of the Gelug Sect. As a lay official, Sanggyi Gyamco's control over the soul boy confirmation of Dalai Lama would definitely lead to tougher conflicts. Due to these important factors, the goal of the 5th Dalai Lama and Sanggyi Gyamco eventually came to nothing despite their careful arrangements, and the result became one of the major sources of subsequent conflicts and wars.

VI. Conflicts on the Confirmation of the 6ᵗʰ Dalai Lama

After the 5ᵗʰ Dalai Lama's demise in 1682, Diba Sanggyi Gyamco withheld the news as previously discussed, declaring that the 5ᵗʰ Dalai Lama was in seclusion studying scriptures and that he was acting on the Dalai Lama's behalf. In the meantime, the holy stupa for the 5ᵗʰ Dalai Lama was under secret construction and the confirmation of his soul boy was being carried out. Memorials and proclamations were still presented to the Qing Emperor in the name of the 5ᵗʰ Dalai Lama.

In 1683, Cangyang Gyamco was born at Moindawang. When he was three, reports on the intelligent things he had done were circulated by local people. Upon receiving these reports, Sanggyi Gyamco indicated that Cangyang Gyamco might be the soul boy of Shalukangqen, the 5ᵗʰ Dalai Lama's teacher, and gave orders to local officials to protect the boy with an intention of confirming him as the soul boy of the 5ᵗʰ Dalai Lama. Later, the soul boy was transferred to Cona, and Sanggyi Gyamco several times sent aides for secret inspection.

According to Sanggyi Gyamco's

Statue of the 6ᵗʰ Dalai Lama (1683-1706), preserved in the Potala Palace.   CHEN ZONTGLIE

record, Cangyang Gyamcoís uncle did not get along well with the boyís parents, and he bribed Zongboin at Nazong, who then deliberately raised difficulties and persecuted Cangyang Gyamcoís family. Things became better after Diba Sanggyi Gyamco sent some attendants to the family.

Cangyang Gyamco began studying language and scriptures at the age of eight. At the time, only few people (including Sanggyi Gyamco) knew that the 5th Dalai Lama had passed away, and Cangyang Gyamco had been determined as his soul boy, even though neither the child nor his parents were aware of this. Outsiders were merely told that the boy might be the soul boy of Shalukangqen. And this became the first case for the Gelug Sect of dealing with the soul boy affairs of the Dalai Lama secretly with the administrative power from lay people.

Although the headman of Hoshot in Lhasa and Emperor Kangxi had cast some doubts on the death of the 5th Dalai Lama, they could not oppose the soul boy affairs without evidence. It was as late as 1696 before Emperor Kangxi learnt of the 5th Dalai Lama's demise from the people at Zunggar when he was conquering Gandain. He then issued an edict, calling Diba Sanggyi Gyamco to account over the matter. He had to report to the emperor that the 5th Dalai Lama had been dead many years, and his

<<*Mural in the Potala Palace: Lazang Khan (right) and Diba Sangyi Gyamco.*
CHEN ZONTGLIE

soul boy was already 15 years of age, with the sitting-in-the-bed ceremony scheduled to be held in the following October. Under such circumstances, Emperor Kangxi had no alternative but to agree to the confirmation by Sanggyi Gyamco, accepting Cangyang Gyamco as the soul boy of the 5th Dalai Lama. Back in 1693, Diba Sanggyi Gyamco wrote a memorial to Emperor Kangxi in the name of the 5th Dalai Lama, claiming that he was old, and a lot of important issues had been transferred to Diba Sanggyi Gyamco, whom he had promoted several years earlier. He requested Emperor Kangxi to grant Diba Sanggyi Gyamco a title and a seal of authority, which would demonstrate royal favor and be beneficial for the Diba to give administrative orders. Although Emperor Kangxi knew nothing about the 5th Dalai Lama's death then, and the Tibetan and Mongolian monks acting

> Statue of the 7th Dalai Lama (1708-1757), preserved in the Potala Palace.　　CHEN ZONTGLIE

as messengers failed to inform him of the truth, Emperor Kangxi had suspicions of Diba Sanggyi Gyamco. However, the memorial was written in the name of the 5th Dalai Lama, so it was difficult to countermand it. After some deliberation, Emperor Kangxi conferred the title of Prince on Sanggyi Gyamco, and granted him a golden seal of authority.

In May 1697, Cangyang Gyamco was welcomed to Nanggarze from Cona. In September, the 5th Panchen Erdeni started out from Xigaze to interview Cangyang Gyamco at Nanggarze, where he tonsured Cangyang Gyamco, held a *sramanera* (Buddhist novice) ceremony for him, and gave him the Buddhist monastic name of Cangyang Gyamco. Then, Cangyang

^^ *Stone tablet Qing Emperor Kangxi erected in Lhasa to mark the Qing Troops' success to beat Zungar invaders. It is preserved in the Potala Palace.*
CHEN ZONTGLIE

Gyamco and the 5th Panchen went to Lhasa. On the lantern festival on October 25th, the sitting-in-the-bed ceremony was held for the 6th Dalai Lama Cangyang Gyamco at Potala Palace, with Hoshot Mongol Khan Dalaikhan and Sanggyi Gyamco and others being present. The 2nd Living Buddha Zanggyia Ngawang Qoidain was sent by Emperor Kangxi from Beijing to Lhasa to participate in the ceremony and give presents to the 6th Dalai Lama, which marked the first time for a Qing Emperor to be involved in the soul boy affairs of the Dalai Lama. The emperor also sent people to attend the sitting-in-the-bed ceremony.

Lhazang Khan took over as Khan of Hoshot in 1703 and continuously governed Tibet, where relations with Diba Sanggyi Gyamco gradually worsened. To prevent the conflict from worsening, in the year when Lhazang Khan became Khan, he renounced his position as Disi, with his son—Ngawang Renqen (Chosa)—assuming it and working together with Lhazang Khan. Actually, Sanggyi Gyamco still held real power.

In 1705, the conflict between Diba Sanggyi Gyamco and Lhazang Khan broke out, and the former was captured and killed. The 6th Dalai Lama Cangyang Gyamco immediately became the center of the conflict between the Mongolian and Tibetan leadership, which involved the issue of whether the confirmation of the soul boy was legal and had been acknowledged. Lhazang Khan claimed that Cangyang Gyamco was not the real soul boy of the 6th Dalai Lama considering the facts that he was confirmed solely by Sanggyi Gyamco by breaking the commandments. Cangyang Gyamco was banished and sent to Beijing under guard, and passed away at Gonggar Nur beside Qinghai Lake. Onc legend said he did not pass away, but fled from Qinghai Lake and lived in Gansu, Qinghai, and Mongolia for a long period of time, and ultimately died at Alashan in Inner Mongolia, but this story is hardly credible.

Lhazang Khan chose Yishi Gyamco as the soul boy of the 5th Dalai Lama with a view to controlling the power to system of selecting the Dalai Lama. Although Lhazang Khan had been approved by Emperor Kangxi of Qing Dynasty and had won the support from the 5th Panchen Erdeni, the activity of selecting another Dalai Lama was still a source of much trouble. Emperor Kangxi granted a golden seal of authority to Yishi Gyamco and ordered that Cangyang Cyamco be sent to Beijing. Apparently, the em-

The Qing court exercised direct rule over Tibet when it drove the Zungar out of the region. Pholhanas was given the official position as benzi and the chief galoon of the local government of Tibet (Gashag). He was later appointed prefectural prince to be in charge of administrative affairs of Tibet. Pictured here is a portrait of the man in the Sera Monastery.

peror recognized Cangyang Gyamco as a figure previously identified as the Dalai Lama; had he stayed in Tibet, which had once been controlled by the Zunggar, or invited to stay in Xinjiang, the consequences would have been severe. Hence, it was better to keep Cangyang Gyamco under his wing in Beijing. However, the deposition of Cangyang Gyamco brought forward problems. The Mongolian leaders in Qinghai (mostly relatives of Lhazang Khan) and some upper level monks of the three major monasteries in Tibet were against what Lhazang Khan had done, and so, from Litang, came the news that Cangyang Gyamco was staying there.

Getting the news that the soul boy of the Dalai Lama had appeared in Litang, Lhazang Khan sent his trusted men such as Depoin Norbu Wochi, Mongolian Gyianoryan and Dawa Zaisang to Litang on a secret ìinvestigationî.

The Mongolian leader in Qinghai did not accept Yishi Gyamco as the Dalai Lama and sent his men to Litang in the Kham area to seek the intelligent child named Galsang Gyamco, who was already being promoted by local lay people and monks and some people of the three major monasteries in Lhasa as the soul boy of Cangyang Gyamco, and who was invited to Qinghai. The Qing Dynasty at the time had no direct control over the political and religious affairs in Qinghai and Tibet and it was inappropriate to express a clear attitude on the dispute between Lhazang Khan and the

Mongolian leader in Qinghai. All that could be done was to order the Mongolian leader in Qinghai to send Galsang Gyamco to reside in the Tar Monastery in Qinghai to await developments in the political situation in Qinghai and Tibet.

Cekuang Alabutan, of the Zunggar tribe, also butted into the issue by selecting yet another soul boy candidate in order to try and control Tibet. Part of his strategy was to achieve a marriage between his daughter and the son of Lhazang Khan. In 1617, Cekuang Alabutan dispatched a military force into Tibet in the name of escorting his daughter and son-in-law to Tibet, where he killed Lhazang Khan in a sudden attack. The Dalai Lama Yishi Gyamco, who was supported by Lhazang Khan, was naturally deposed by the Zunggar military force.

Another important part of Cekuang Alabutan's strategy was that he proclaimed widely that his forces were escorting the soul boy of Cangyang Gyamco to Lhasa to restore the Gelug Sect and the position of the real Dalai Lama, in an effort to win the support of the monks and lay people in Tibet. But the platoon sent by Zunggar to the Tar Monastery in Qinghai to seize Galsang Gyamco was defeated by a Qing military force on the way. The seizure of Lhasa by the Zunggari was witnessed by the Jesuit priest Ippolito Desideri, who wrote: "He gave orders to ransack Lhasa. The monks who joined his forces

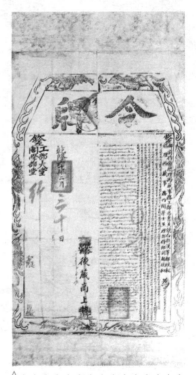

Tablet of order from the Qing High Commissioner in Tibet.
CHEN ZONTGLIE

*portrait of Qing Emperor Qianlong the emperor
bestowed to the 7th Dalai Lama.   CHEN ZONTGLIE*

were greedy and cruel robbers. They carried weapons and broke into the houses of local people or even their cahoots. They also intruded into the monasteries to ransack the stored and hidden treasures. This was not all. They broke into the people's houses again and again, insulting and beating cruelly the men and women, or the young and the old, or hanging them from the roof beams for torture, forcing them to tell where they had hid their valuables. The looting lasted for two days and nights."

"The Tartars ransacked the Potala Palace.... and the private bedroom of Dalai Lama, the important Buddhist halls of the palace ."The plunder and slaughter carried out by the Zunggar soldiers brought down on them the curse from the monks and lay people in Tibet and the protest from local power headed by Khangchennas and Pholhanas. Khangchennas and Pholhanas, as well as the noble Ngaphodpa in the Lhasa area, sent messengers to the Qing Court to report on the political situation of Tibet and plead for troops to be sent to drive out the Zunggari forces.

In order to send military forces to Tibet and win the support of the monks and lay people in Tibet as well as the Mongolian leader in Qinghai, the Qing Dynasty finally accepted the Dalai Lama identity of Galsang Gyamco. On May 26, 1720 (April 20 according to lunar calendar, the 20th day of the third Tibetan month), Emperor Kangxi dispatched his 14th Prince to the Tar Monastery in Qinghai and granted a golden seal of authority and golden sheets of confirmation along with abundant gifts to Galsang Gyamco. He, in turn, knelt down for acceptance and declared that he expected to thank the emperor personally by going to Beijing.

On the 150 tael golden sheets of confirmation there are carved characters in Manchu, Mongolian and Tibetan languages, whose rough meaning can still be identified in the copies of memorials to the throne for the military-political affairs setup preserved in the China No.1 History Archives: "The Dalai Lama, who studied intensively the scriptures from a child, is deeply trusted by all tribes. The royal court grants him the seal and sheets as an honor of being the 6th Dalai Lama." Here, Emperor Kangxi directly took the new soul boy as the successor of the 5th Dalai Lama, denying the claim of Cangyang Cyamco as decided by Sanggyi Gyamco, and rejecting the candidate previously supported by the Qing Dynasty-honored Lhazang Khan.

However, the monks and lay people still regarded Cangyang Gyamco as the 6th Dalai Lama and the new soul boy born at Litang as his soul boy, i.e. the 7th Dalai Lama. Not until 60 years later, when the 6th Panchen Erdeni came to Chengde to congratulate Emperor Qianlong on his 70th birthday in 1780 (the 45th year of the reign), did the emperor officially accept Gyiangbai Gyamco, the soul boy of Galsang Gyamco as the 8th Dalai Lama according to the will of Tibetan people, and granting him the jade sheets of confirmation and jade seal of authority. Thus Galsang Gyamco naturally became the 7th Dalai Lama in the records of Qing Dynasty.

VII. The Search and Confirmation of the 8th Dalai Lama

The military escort provided by the Qing Dynasty accompanied Galsang Gyamco to Tibet for the sitting-in-the-bed ceremony. With the army's entry into Tibet, the Qing Court deposed Hoshot Khan and established its direct rule over the territory. Before long, the Mongolian leader Norbu Tsangdainjin in Qinghai took the lead in supporting Galsang Gyamco as the Dalai Lama, as a means of taking over the ruling position of Hoshot Khan in Tibet. When The Qing Dynasty rejected him, he stirred up a rebellion by Mongolians in Qinghai against the Qing Dynasty. The imperial court took decisive measures to suppress the uprising led by Norbu Tsangdainjin in Qinghai and obtained direct rule over the region.

Statue of the 8th Dalai (1758-1804), preserved in the Potala Palace.
CHEN ZONTGLIE

After getting rid of the Zunggari forces, the Qing Dynasty set up its direct control over Tibet and appointed Khangchennas from among the Tibetan nobles as the head of Galoon officials. However, the Galoon officials in power soon became embroiled in conflicts. In 1727, the Lhasa area-born Galoon officials such as Ngaphodpa, Lhungponas and Zharnas instigated internal conflict and killed Khangchennas in a struggle over power and profits. They sought to capture Pholhanas in the Xigaze area. Hearing of this, Pholhanas realized that it was a plot against the central government, so he sent a message to the royal court immediately, while raising troops in the Xigaze area and nearby Ngari. After a fight lasting half a year, Pholhanas captured Lhasa and, with the help of the monks of the three major monasteries, captured Ngaphodpa and his aides, and reported to the Qing Dynasty for a decision on dealing with them. At this moment, the army sent by the Qing Dynasty arrived in Lhasa. Ngaphodpa and his chief aides were beheaded after a joint confirmation. The Qing Court presented its positive view on Pholhanas' merits by honoring him as Bezi and appointed him as the leading Galoon official, and later upgraded him to be a prince holding overall leadership in the local administration of Tibet.

The Qing Dynasty also appointed Garxiba Namu Zhale Serbuten and Ceren Wanggyi as Galoon officials, but the local power fell totally into the hands of Pholhanas. When the father of the 7th Dalai Lama fell out with Pholhanas and sided with the supporters of Ngaphodpa, in order to prevent a repeat of the Zunggar army interfering in Tibetan affairs, Emperor Yongzhen, in 1728, ordered that the residence of the 7th Dalai Lama be moved to the Huiyuan Temple in Taining, Sichuan, and also ordered Soinam Dagyi, the Dalai Lama's father, to come to Beijing. Soinam Dagyi was worried he would be punished in Beijing, but when he proved respectful and submissive after arriving in the capital, the emperor decided that punishing him would have an adverse impact on the 7th Dalai Lama, so instead granted him a ducal title to prevent him from interfering in the political affairs of Tibet. This marked the beginning of the system whereby the relatives of Dalai Lama were honored as dukes by the central government.

The father of the 7th Dalai Lama was also allowed to own houses of Gushri Khan entitled as Sangzhub Phodrang in Lhasa's Barkor Street area , and was given some manors and serfs in Shannan, which became the hereditary property of his family. As a result, his family became an influential noble family called the Sangpo clan in Tibet. Such noble fami-

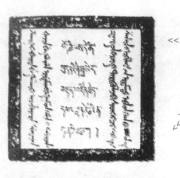

<< *Silver seal of authority Qing Emperor Qianlong bestowed to the 1st Dimo Hutugtu, appointing him to be Regent of Tibet. The seal text in Manchurian, Tibetan and Mongolian reads in part "Seal of Mmanagement over Tibetan Affairs and Yellow Sect doctrines."*   CHEN ZONTGLIE

Qing Emperor Qianlong appointed the 1st Living Buddha Ceimoling as Tibetan Regent, with a seal text.
CHEN ZONTGLIE

lies based on the fathers of Dalai Lamas of different generations were respected as ìYaî families, becoming the grandest among the noble families in Tibet.

The Qing Dynasty also set up the system of High Commissioners in 1727 with the establishment of a High Commissioners' Office in Lhasa, whose occupants stayed there a long time to supervise local political power. The court stationed 2,000 soldiers in Tibet commanded by the High Commissioners. In addition, the Qing Dynasty also settled the geographical limits for Tibet, Qinghai and Sichuan and the administrative sphere for Tibet.

Pholhanas did much meritorious work as a Galoon official and prince. He reformed the post stations to ensure the delivery of government orders and documents. Upon the instruction of Emperor Qianlong, he received the envoy of boiling tea to worship Buddha from Zunggar as approved by the Qing Dynasty. He also expressed his willingness to improve relations with the 7th Dalai Lama and took some measures in this regard. In 1735, the Zunggari threat to Tibet was finally removed and Emperor Yongzhen dispatched Deputy General Fushou and State Tutor

Zanggyia Rubi Dorje to escort the 7th Dalai Lama to return Lhasa.

But once back there, the local administration was still handled by Pholhanas and the Dalai Lama could only manage the religious affairs of the Gelug Sect. In 1746, someone claimed that Dasoiboin Zhakbadayan of the 7th Dalai Lama had instigated his secretary Canggyi to curse Pholhanas. The latter felt this was the extension of the old revenge that had led Ngaphodpa and others to murder Khangchennas; he therefore considered the matter was related to the 7th Dalai Lama. The 7th Dalai Lama denied any involvement, but Pholhanas insisted on making an investigation. The 7th Dalai Lama was discontented with Pholhanas for this reason and expressed to others: "There is no doubt this is against me". From this example we are able to see the deep conflicts between the political and religious leaders in Tibet and that the 7th Dalai Lama had no right to interfere in the political affairs of Tibet when Pholhanas was in power.

Stone tablet Qing Emperor Qianlong erected in Lhasa, to mark Qing trooopsis success to defeat Korgas invaders.   *CHEN ZONTGLIE*

Pholhanas died in 1747 and his son Zhulmut Namo Zhale succeeded him as prince in full administrative control in Tibet. However, after he came to power, he killed his brother stationed in Ngari, and then had dispute with Dalai Lama; he was also hostile to the High Commissioners, blocked the delivery of military letters and tried to contact Zunggar for support.

Since most of the forces of the Qing Dynasty stationed in Tibet had *the 29-article Ordinance for the More Effective Governing of Tibet promulgated by the Qing government in 1793.*

CHEN ZONTGLIE

withdrawn to the hinterland in 1733, Lhasa was again placed in a dangerous situation. In 1751, High Commissioners Fu Qing and Lhabudain first trapped and killed Zhulmut Namo Zhale, but they themselves were murdered by his henchmen and their office was burnt down.

After the incident, the 7th Dalai Lama, using his own religious influence, appointed Gongpandit to handle administrative affairs, arrested the murderers of the High Commissioners and stabilized the situation in Lhasa, while waiting for the Qing Dynasty to send officials for disposal of the various issues.

When the army dispatched by the Qing Dynasty entered Tibet, its leader, led by Viceroy Chelen, after investigation, proposed the 13-article Ordnance for the Governance of Tibet. Emperor Qianlong felt that Zhulmut Namo Zhale had dared to rebel due to Tibetís ìwide territory, strong military forces and centralized powerî and ìthat the Galoon officialsí affairs were greatly concerned with their powerî. The Qing Government, to deal with the problem once and for all, decided to seize the chance after suppressing the rebellion to reform the local political system by canceling the system of princely sole control over Tibetan affairs. Instead, the Dalai Lama was the leader of Gaxag government controlling the administration of Tibet, with power distributed to four Galoon officials (one monk and three lay people).

All Galoon officials were equal in position. In case of any event, they had to report to the High Commissioners and Dalai Lama for instruction. They jointly handled the various affairs of the locality without being a law unto themselves. Meanwhile, they were under the supervision of the High Commissioners. The latter also had direct control over the 39-Tribe Area and Damo (Damxung) Mongol originally administrated by Zhulmut Namo Zhale.

In 1754 (the Tibetan Year of Wooden Dog), the 7th Dalai Lama set up Zelhozha (Potala Palace school for the training of monk officials), which was moved by the 8th Dalai Lama into the Potala Palace itself in May 1788 (the Tibetan Year of Earth Monkey). In 1794 (the Tibetan Year of Wooden Tiger), the 8th Dalai Lama worked out a school rule, which was incorporated into the rules for monk official schools by the 13th Dalai Lama on May 26, 1932 (the Tibetan Year of Water Monkey). It was from the time of the 7th Dalai Lama that a large number of monk officials were sent to the Gaxag government and various sects to hold various posts. Besides calligraphy and grammar, the schools for the training of monk officials also opened such courses as poetry, calendaring and Sanskrit. The monks that had been trained in these schools would be

Memorial tablet reading "Long live the emperor!" the 7th Dalai Lama worshipped in the Potala Palace.
CHEN ZONTGLIE

the officials of the local governments of Tibet at different levels as the disciples of Dalai Lama, which played a significant role in consolidating the religious and temporal administration system of Tibet and the position of the Dalai Lama.

The 7th Dalai died in 1757. When Emperor Qianlong received the news, he dispatched immediately the 3rd Zanggyia Hutogtu to Tibet to look for and confirm the soul boy. Meanwhile, the emperor appointed Dimo Living Buddha Ngawang Jambei Deleg Gyamco as Regent to handle the religious and temporal affairs in Tibet.

In searching for the soul boy, the Buddhist guardian would be invited to offer some instruction as to where the soul boy was born and could be found. Because the directions advised by the four Buddhist guardians differed, the soul boys found in the Xigaze area could not be affirmed, and thus dispute was aroused.

Records show that the arguments about the soul boy of the 7th Dalai Lama were particularly fiery. Even Zanggyia Rubi Dorje, a grand Living Buddha authorized by Emperor Qianlong, felt it was so hard to come to a decision that he decided to invite the 6th Panchen Erdeni to Lhasa, and ask for the advice of the living Buddha Regent Dimo by briefing him about the soul boy search.

The 6th Panchen Erdeni met Zanggyia Rubi Dorje and insisted that the child born in Tobugyia in the Xigaze area should be the soul boy. After another review, the 3rd Zanggyia returned to Beijing to report to Emperor Qianlong. In January 1761, with the emperorís approval, the soul boy was brought to Tashilhungpo Monastery to be tonsured and given the name Gyiangbai Gyamco by the 6th Panchen Erdeni.

Gyangbai Gyamco was invited to Lhasa to live in the Dewagyia Monastery in Nytang, where he was greeted by Regent Dimo Hutogtu, the High Commissioners, leaders of the three major monasteries and Galoon officials. The High Commissioners submitted in March a request to the emperor for the sitting-in-the-bed, and received the permission in May; at the same time, Purbujo Lama Ngawang Qamba, Gyangze and Prince of Dharma Xaqoinba Ngawang Qoizha, were appointed as sutra teachers.

In July 1762, the sitting-in-the-bed ceremony was held in the Potala Palace for the enthronement of the 8th Dalai Lama. Emperor Qianlong specially appointed a Gurkhas Mongol Prince and Ngagyia Hutogtu of the Tar Monastery in Qinghai to go to Lhasa to attend the ceremony. The 6th Panchen Erdeni was also present. The father of the 8th Dalai Lama was granted a dukedom by the Qing government, and was given manors and serfs by the Gaxag government, thereby creating the new Lhalu clan in Tibet.

Although the soul boy of 7th Dalai Lama was selected and confirmed by the 6th Panchen Erdeni and Zanggyia Rubi Dorje of the Gelug Sect as authorized by Emperor Qianlong, so that there were no severe conflicts among the upper classes of monks and common people, still some problems were created. According to the *Biography of Zanggyia State Tutor Rubi Dorje,* even after sitting-in-the-bed ceremony, a few monks of the Gelug Sect insisted that a boy born in Shannan was the real soul boy, and urged the people to deny Gyiangbai Gyamco the right to be the 8th Dalai Lama.

Emperor Qianlong was angered by the news, and decided to arrest these monks and bring them to Beijing, but he was dissuaded by Zanggyia Rubi Dorje. Finally, he made the boy from Shannan and his tutor chamberlains to the Panchen Erdeni in the Tashilhungpo Monastery, where they could be kept under surveillance, to safeguard Tibet from disturbance.

VIII. Introduction of the System of Drawing a Lot From the Golden Urn to Determine the Soul Boys of Late Living Buddhas

From 1751, the situation in Tibet gradually became stable. The Qing government reinforced its administration over Tibet, and, accordingly, the Tibetan-inhabited areas in northwest and southwest, since they had historically close relations with Tibet.

In the northwest, the Qing government appointed a Xining Affairs Minister to take care of the Qinghai army garrison, the provisions and funds for the troops, and post station and transportation matters.

In the southwest, more attention was given to the control and administration of transportation lines from Sichuan and Yunnan to Tibet. Dimo Living Buddha Ngawang Jambei Deleg Gyamco passed away in 1777, and the Qing government sent Living Buddha Ceimoling who was then the abbot of Yonghegong Lamasery in Beijing, to Tibet as Regent. It was during that period that the power system of Dalai Lama, High Commissioners and Regent was established.

The 6th Panchen Erdeni was invited to Beijing in 1779, and he reached Rehe in August 1780 to take part in the celebration of Emperor Qianlongís 70th birthday before going on to Beijing. He died of disease in Huangsi Temple, Beijing, at the end of October. Emperor Qianlong decreed the first month of the lunar new year of 1781, or the 46th year of his reign, that the 8th Dalai Lama should

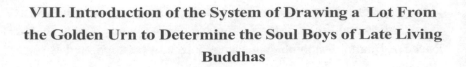

>> *Golden urn Qing Emperor Qianlong gave to Tibet for the determining of soul boy of the late Dalai Lama or the Panchen Erdeni. CHEN ZONTGLIE*

rule the region, and, following the convention of the last Dalai Lama, he undergo formal investiture as the Dalai Lama, Overseer of the Buddhist Faith on Earth Under the Great Benevolent Self-subsisting Buddha of Western Paradise. The 8th Dalai Lama came to power in 1784. When Zanggyia State Tutor Rubi Dorje died in 1786, the Qing government called Living Buddha Ceimoling back to Beijing, and appointed him Jilung Hutogtu Regent to help the Dalai Lama with local affairs.

After 40 years of stability, Tibet, with its intrinsic contradiction of feudal serfdom and the decline of power of the Qing Dynasty as Emperor Qianlong aged, again faced turbulence. Twice, Gurkhas from Nepal invaded Tibet.

In 1788-1789, the 53rd-54th years of the reign of Emperor Qianlong, the first invasion occurred as a result of so-called local Tibetan officials levying fees on Gurkha merchants and craftsmen, and the fact that Tibet continually supported Mengzehsiong against the Gurkhas. The Gurkha army took Jilung in Nylam quickly, and besieged Zongka. High Commissioner Qingling reported to the central government saying that he had insufficient troops to resist. Qingling himself headed the soldiers who went to Tashilhungpo Monastery to take care of the Panchen Erdeni and provide food supplies for the front. Emperor Qianlong, therefore, ordered Yue Hui, the Chengdu General, and Counselor of Sichuan Prefecture based in Chengdu to lead troops into Tibet to counterattack. Also, the Minister in Charge of Religious Affairs in Mongolia and Tibet, Bazhong, was asked to enter Tibet to deal with the situation. Bazhong dispatched Galoon official Dainjin Banzhol to negotiate peace, who then privately promised the Gurkhas that Tibet would pay silver 480 kg for their evacuation from Nylam, Zongka and Jilung. Bazhong then reported to Emperor Qianlong that Tibet was clear of

Gurkhas and their king would pay tribute to the Qing government. The war was over.

In the summer of 1791, the seven month of the 56th year of the reign of Emperor Qianlong, the Gurkhas again took Nylam because had Tibet refused to pay the promised war compensation. The reason why Gurkhas twice started war within such a short period was closely related to the greedy brother of the 6th Panchen Erdeni. He was also a living Buddha belonging to the Red-Hat system with the religious name of Quzhub Gyamco (1738-1791). In 1779, when the 6th Panchen Erdeni went to Rehe to offer congratulations on Emperor Qianlong's birthday, he received a large amount of money and treasure and livestock; also, he got plentiful largesse from the Emperor in Beijing. After his death, all his effects passed into his brother's hand. He only gave a portion of the livestock to the Tashilhungpo Monastery, and kept the rest. He abetted the king of the Gurkhas to attack the Tashilhungpo Monastery. Gurkhas crossed over the birder into Tibet with no resistance offered at all. High Commissioner Baotai moved the 7th Panchen Erdeni to Lhasa at his own discretion "for the sake of his security" in September, thus causing lay people and monks of the Tashilhungpo Monastery to lose heart. The Sorcerer Lama Zezhong and abbots of Zhacang alleged that god had given an indication that they should not fight against the enemy. Zongpa Hutogtu took the treasure and ran away, so that the people were not organized to resist. Some 1000 Gurkhas without any losses thus took the Tashilhungpo Monastery and committed robbery. A few dozen Qing soldiers continued to hold the castle on the top of Zongshan Hill in Xigaze, thus stopping the Gurkhas from advancing further. In October, the Gurkhas took their loot and evacuated Xigaze to go to Nylam.

The Qing government appointed Fukang'an as Grand General,

and Hailancha and Kuilin as counselors to head the counterattacking troops. When they entered Tibet, the 8th Dalai Lama and Jilung Hutogtu and various Galoon officials all expressed their willingness to help with provisions. Food for the army would be provided by the Dalai Lama's own warehouse, Tashilhungpo Monastery, the monasteries of the Sagya Sect and all noble class and officials, and the balance would come from public collection. With the help of Tibetan monks and lay people, Fukangían led nearly 20,000 troops to Kathmandu, forcing the Gurkhas to surrender. They returned their loot and promised not to intrude into Tibet any more, and pay tribute on time. They also returned the bones and ashes of dead Living Buddhas of the Red-Hat System.

Closely following this, the Qing government punished people for their activities in the war. All 103 red-hat lamas were forced to convert to the Yellow Sect under the administration of three major monasteries. Emperor Qianlong commanded the 6th Panchen's brother Zongpa Hutogtu (the Tashilhungpo Monastery Zhasake Lama Lobsang Jinba) who fled when Gurkhas attacked the Tashilhungpo Monastery be sent under guard to Beijing for sentencing. Zizhong Lama and others who urged the invasion not be resisted were seized and taken to Lhasa to be punished in public. The Yangbajain Monastery vested in Jilung Hutogtu, and monks under the administration of three major monasteries. Thereafter the Red-Hat Yangbajain Monastery was converted to the Gelug Sect.

In view of the problems with regard to the Tibetan system, the Qing government ordered Fukang'an to discuss and work out an ordinance for the more effective governing of the region. Fukang'an met with the 8th Dalai Lama and the 7th Panchen Erdeni successively, telling them of his idea about the statute. They both agreed. In 1793, with the approval of the Qing government, the Ordinance for the More Effective Governing of Tibet was issued. It contained 29 articles, including the following:

1. High Commissioners shall supervise all Tibetan affaires with equal power held by the Dalai Lama and Panchen Erdeni on the basis of consultation. All officials, from Galoon officials down to the lowest level, and Living Buddhas, shall obey the High Commissioners' order; the High Commissioners together with the Dalai Lama shall determine and report to the Emperor for ratification the appointment of officials such as Galoon officials, Depoin, Zeben, Qianzu Relatives of the Dalai Lama and the Panchen Erdeni shall not intervene in political affairs while they live. Zongboin of border areas shall be selected from among junior Zongboins and capable soldiers; officials be chosen based on their competence and contribution, not only on their parentage. The use of Ula shall be allowed with tickets stampedwith seals of the High Commissioners and Dalai Lama on them.

2. Soul boy of the Dalai Lama, Panchen Erdeni or other grand Living Buddhas should be determined through the method of drawing lot from the golden urn; the abbot and Living Buddha of large monasteries shall be determined by consultation between the Dalai Lama, High Commissioners and Jilung Hutogtu (namely Regent), given license with seals of the above three; Living Buddha and Lama from monasteries under the administration of Dalai Lama shall all be listed for reference; dukes coming to invite a Tibetan Living Buddha shall get formal letters from the Xining Minister to the High Commissioners, and passes from High Commissioners to the Xining Minister for reference. Living Buddhas traveling needs a pass as well, or they will be punished.

3. Founding Emperor Qianlong coins and reinforcing currency

control; High Commissioners audit the Dalai Lama and Panchen Erdeniís commercial expenses, relieving and freeing people of the Xigaze area from tax and corvee; fair transactions; tax and corvee free licenses shall be issued by High Commissioners and Dalai Lama. Living Buddha and Lamaís salary shall not be advanced.

4. The official local military force (the Tibetan Army) was established for units to be stationed in various important places in the Xigaze area, and officials were appointed to the general leadership. The number of soldiers and promotion system controlled by officers such as Depoin, Ruboin, Gyiaboin and Dingboin was specified. The High Commissioners were to inspect the arrays at sites in the Xigaze area in both spring and autumn.

5.The times that Nepalese merchants and Kashmir merchants came to Tibet were limited for strengthening management. The artisans and others sent by the Dalai Lama to Nepal had tot have road permits approved by the High Commissioners and they had to return within a specified time. Boundary tablets were erected at the important places between Tibet and the Gurkha controlled areas (Nepal) with reinforced patrols. The letters of the Dalai Lama sent to and received from foreign countries had to be carefully checked by the High Commissioners. The import and export tariff levied in Jilung and Nylam could not be increased without the permission of the High Commissioners.

Emperor Qianlong paid much attention to the management of affairs related to the soul boy of the Living Buddha. To check abuses in looking for and confirming the soul boy, the first item of the 29-article Ordinance for the More Effective Governing of Tibet established a system of drawing lots from the golden urn, i.e. "when looking for a living Buddha and the soul boy of Hutogtu, the four Buddhist guardians must be asked to practice divination to confirm the soul boy according to the tradition of Tibetan people", which inevitably brought about problems. The emperor especially granted a gold urn to help the Yellow Sect prosper. Whenever the looking for and confirming of a soul boy occurred, the four Buddhist guardians would be invited to write the names and birth dates of the soul boys on the lots in the Manchu, Chinese and Tibetan languages, and then put them into the urn. True learned living Buddha would be selected to pray for seven days and the Hutogtus and High Commissioners would carry out official confirmation before the statue of Sakyamuni at Jokhang Monastery. Providing only one soul boy was found, a lot carrying the soul boy's name and one blank lot had to be put into the urn together. If the blank lot was drawn, the found child could not be confirmed as the soul boy and the search had to begin again. The Dalai Lama and Panchen Erdeni have to behave like teacher and student in choosing each others soul boy. Each of them shall write the names of the soul boy candidates of the other in Manchu, Chinese and Tibet languages on the lots.

With regard to management over Tibetan Buddhism, there were the following stipulations:

Article 2: People who come from Bhutan and Mengzehsiong to worship Buddha in Lhasa must be reported, too. When a foreigner is returning to his own country, he will be controlled and inspected by Zongboins in different places. The people sent by the Dalai Lama to Nepal for building a statue of Buddha and worship must have road permits signed by the High Commissioners. If they are unable to return in due time, the High Commissioners shall write to the King of the Gurkhas. Handling affairs in such a manner can either clarify boundary affairs or benefit Tibet.

Article 8:The income and expenses of the Dalai Lama and the Panchen Erdeni were not approved by High Commissioners in previous times. The management of the income and expenses of the Dalai Lama and the Panchen Erdeni by their relatives and suites inevitably brings about embezzlement. The emperor, therefore, has ordered the High Commissioners to examine and verify the accounting and report to the emperor in both spring and winter each year. In case of any concealment and embezzlement, penalty should be imposed immediately.î

Article 10: When the High Commissioners supervise and handle affairs in Tibet, they shall have equal position with the Dalai Lama and Panchen Erdeni, disposing of political affairs together through discussion. All chiefs and officials as well as living Buddhas under Galoon officials are subject to the leadership of the High Commissioners and, grand or not, they have to obey them. All affairs of Tashilhungpo Monastery are to be handled by the abbot when the Panchen Erdeni is still young. But for justice, all special affairs shall be reported to the High Commissioners first, so they can dispose of them when they make a tour to the places for inspection.

Article 11: The staff of Tashilhungpo Monastery are all monks, who had no titles in the past and the number of monks was undefined. From now on, when there is a vacancy for the position of Qianzu, Soiboin Lama (in charge of diet) and Sengboin Lama (in charge of bedrooms) shall be selected to fill it. When there is a vacancy for the position of Soiboin, a Zezong will be appointed to fill it. When there is a vacancy for the position of Sengboin, a Zongnyi will be appointed to fill it. No free promotion is allowed. There are few villages that are subject to the control of Tashilhungpo Monastery and there are no important sects in the boundary places. All Qianzu, Soiboin, Sengboin and Zongboin are to be considered and appointed by the Panchen Erdeni and the High Commissioners according to the system prevailing in the Lhasa area. As for the insignificant staff handling trivial affairs such as the supply of butter, *zanba* and firewood, they can be appointed by the Panchen Erdeni personally according to their skills. Old routines can be referred to for the provision of Ula corvee labor.

Article 12: The accompanying officials of the Dalai Lama and Panchen Erdeni were all related to them in the past. For example, the Dalai Lama's uncle and the Panchen Erdeni's father Bandain Tuzhub were all promoted privately. The Dalai Lama's brother Lobsang Gedain Zhuba broke the rules many a time with the influence of the Dalai Lama. Henceforth, according to the will of the monks and lay people in Tashilhungpo, and the people at different levels in Tibet, the relatives of the Dalai Lama and Panchen Erdeni are not allowed to handle government affairs when the latter are alive. After their demise, these relatives, if any, can be granted suitable posts according to their skills.

Article 14: In future, when the Gurkhas want to send somebody to visit the Dalai Lama and the High Commissioners, the letter for response must be written according to the instruction of the High Commissioners. As for important affairs at the border, they have to be handled according to the instructions of the High Commissioners. The gifts presented by foreign visitors must be inspected by the High Commissioners. Bhutan, which was granted an honorific title by the emperor, though different in terms of religious sect, sends people each year to present contributions to the Dalai Lama. Sikkim, Zongba and Mengtang also sent contributions to the Dalai Lama and Panchen Erdeni each year. No effort shall be made to stop these contributions, however, careful inspection shall be carried out. When foreign visitors come to

Tibet, the Zongboin chiefs of border counties shall register the number involved and report to the High Commissioners. After being inspected by the Han officials in Gyangze and Tingri, they can be allowed to head for Lhasa. The letters sent to the Dalai Lama and others from foreign countries must be translated and submitted to the High Commissioners for inspection; the High Commissioners shall write carefully a letter of response to be carried back by the visitors.

Article 18: The Abbot is the head of each monastery, who shall be learned with excellent virtues. As investigated recently, the living Buddhas of the major monasteries possess many manors and since they enjoy the worship of the people, they have lots of contributors. In addition with the benefits obtained from trade, they become greedy for money and goods and are unqualified for their posts. It is ruled that, in future, the abbot of each major monastery, the living Buddha, is to be determined through the discussion between the Dalai Lama, the High Commissioners and the Jilung Hutogtu, and to whom a permit with their seals is to be granted. The selection of a living Buddha for the post of abbot for a small monastery, it can be decided by the Dalai Lama following the old customs.

Article 22: The living Buddhas and Lamas of monasteries controlled by the Dalai Lama shall be listed in a book. Galoon officials are responsible to make a book with detailed information of the households of the villages that are subject to each Hutogtu in Tibet. The office of the High Commissioners and the Dalai Lama each has a copy of the books for convenience of inspection. From now on, once it is found that any lama of any monastery is traveling without a permit, the abbot and Zhasa and other major personnel will be subject to punishment.î

Article 23: îThe princes and dukes of Qinghai and Mongol sent for learned living Buddhas to recite scriptures and pray at their homes. Some were approved by the High Commissioners; but, some went there secretly and are hard to be identified. In future, when the princes and dukes of Qinghai and Mongol invite living Buddhas of Tibet, the minister of Xining has to write a letter to the High Commissioners to grant road permits along with letters to the minister of Xining for the convenience of inspection. The living Buddhas who are to worship Buddhas in other countries have to obtain road permits first before setting out. In case of violation, the abbot and major personnel are to be punished.

Article 28: According to the old rules, money to support living Buddhas and Lamas was provided at a certain time, but, in recent years, the money was provided ahead of schedule. From now on, the money shall be provided at the specific time and the payments ahead of schedule shall be avoided completely. The Jilung Hutogtu is expected to carry out the investigation immediately. In case of finding that the support money is provided ahead of schedule or the money has not been provided completely, the person in charge is to be punished.

In September 1792, the emperor sent people to carry a golden urn to Lhasa, ruling publicly that the central government had decided the soul boy of a living Buddha had to be determined by drawing a lot from it. When the golden urn reached Lhasa, it was warmly welcomed by the 8th Dalai Lama and other monks and lay people in Tibet. As for how to implement the 29-article ordinance, the 8th Dalai Lama enacted the *Declaration of the Year of Water Buffalo* soon after he received the imperial edict on the lot drawing system enforced by the emperor. The declaration read: The emperor loves the people of Tibet, is attentive to the Yellow Sect of Master Zongkapa and has been expecting to become a monk. In return, we should pray more for the emperor according to the instruction of the emperor, the search for the real soul boy is to develop the Yellow Sect. The emperor granted especially a golden urn that was carried here by special people. The golden urn is to be set up in front of the statue of Zongkapa of the Jokhang Monastery. No matter which lama or living Buddha is born in Tibet in future, his age, birth date and name are to be written on a lot and reported to the Dalai Lama and High Commissioner, meanwhile inviting the deities for instruction. When there are several soul boy candidates, their ages, birth dates and names are to be written on the lots and put into the golden urn together. I will lead some learned lamas to pray to Master Zongkapa, and then the High Commissioners are to be invited to Lhadrang to draw a lot publicly. The one whose name is shown on the drawn lot is the real soul boy. In addition, when only one soul boy has been found after inviting deities to descend, his name is to be written on a lot as it is. With the same method, it will be put into the urn with those that bear no name for lot drawing. When the drawn lot is blank, it indicates that the child is not a real reincarnated soul boy and under this circumstance, a new soul boy has to be found. From now on, if there is any soul boy that has been determined by following the old rules, related people will be punished severely.

After the system of drawing a lot from the golden urn had been released, initial practice was soon after carried out in some parts of the Mongolian and Tibetan areas. In February 1793, High Commissioners He Ling sent a report to the emperor, saying: "Nine soul boy candidates were found for Sunba Hutogtu were escorted here from Xining". In the past, their names would be sent to the Dalai Lama and the Panchen Erdeni for nomination. Now, since we have the golden urn, the names of soul boy candidates are written on the lots and put into the golden urn for trial drawing. The Dalai Lama went to the Jokhang Monastery and we supervised people who wrote names of the soul boy candidates on lots which would be put into the golden urn".

After Emperor Qianlong gave up his throne in 1795, he went through the rituals for him to enter the monkhood. In 1798, the 8th Dalai Lama enshrined the portrait of Emperor Qianlong in the Potala Palace. The *Biography of the 8th Dalai Lama* reads, "To bless the people in Tibet, the emperor granted his portrait as an icon worshiped by the Han and Tibetan People. The Dalai Lama has decided to build an excellent house to worship the portrait of Emperor Qianlong." During the period of the 7th Dalai Lama, the memorial tablet of Emperor Kangxi was also enshrined in the hall. Since the system for drawing lot from the golden urn to determine the soul boy of a Living Buddha was introduced by Emperor Qianlong, some important activities of drawing lot from the golden urn to determine the soul boy of Dalai Lama or Panchen Erdeni were conducted before the portrait and memorial tablet of the emperors.

IX. The Confirmation of the 9th Dalai Lama

At the beginning of 1804, the 8th Dalai Lama became seriously ill, and the Gaxag government reported this to the imperial court through the High Commissioners. However, the imperial ministers and physicians dispatched by the Emperor had only arrived in Chengdu, Sichuan, when the news came that the Dalai Lama had passed away. Upon being informed of this in a memorial, the Emperor requested the ministers to continue heading for Tibet and condole with local people on the Dalai Lama's demise in line with Han customs. In the seventh lunar month of that year, just after the 8th Dalai Lama's demise, Emperor Jiaqing installed the Living Buddha Jilung Dainbei Gungbo as Regent, and gave the order to seek the soul boy.

This marked the first time for Qing Empire to seek the soul boy for such a leading Living Buddha as the Dalai Lama since the enactment of

^ *Statue of the 9th Dalai Lama (1805-1815) preserved in the Potala Palace.* *CHEN ZONTGLIE*

the 29-article Ordinance for the More Effective Governing of Tibet. The search and confirmation of Dalai Lama's soul boy, however, were still deeply influenced by previous customs. At first, many distinctive characteristics had been detected in a boy born in Dengke, Sichuan, in 1805. After consulting with four Galoon officials, Jilung Living Buddha Dainbei Gungbo sent an assistant named Raodain Gyamco to Beijing in 1807, reporting to Emperor Jiaqing about the boy. In September of the same year, the soul boy and his father were invited to the Caigungtang Monastery to await the emperor's final decision through the High Commissioners. Although two more intelligent boys had been found, Regent Jilung firmly held that the child born in Dengke was definitely the right one. With a view to persuading the public, he provided offerings in the Sunlight Hall and invited the Great Protector of the Buddha dharma on the first day of the 10th lunar month. Regent Jilung, four Galoon officials, Soiboin abbot, Sengboin abbot and Qoiboin abbot inquired: "The confirmation of the Dalai Lama's soul boy is still in dispute. Please give us a clear indication." The Great Protector replied: " A right image is in the arm of Mother Toinzhub Zholma." Then Panchen turned to Lhamojam divine master Tshang-pa for augury, and got the same answer. Toinzhub Zholma was none other than the name of the Dengke boy's mother of the boy born in Dengke. Later, the Regent invited the High Commissioners, Galoon officials and other monks and lay people to the Caigungtang Monastery, asking the soul boy in the Grand Sutra Hall to identify the late Dalai Lamaís belongings. The late Dalai Lama's image, the images of Tara and Zongkapa that had been carried by Atisa, a bell pestle and some other things were first presented, with a real and a false one for each. When the soul boy was asked to distinguish real from false, he merrily chanted: iThis is mine, and this is mine.

On the 26th day of the 10th lunar month, the High Commissioners wrote a memorial to the throne in the presence of all Lamas and officials, and presented it to the emperor, which read: "The soul boy well and truly made out all the images and belongings, and behaved distinctively. "

After the inspection carried out by the High Commissioners, the Panchen Erdeni and the Regent, as well as the Gaxag government, were required to confirm the child as the soul boy of the 5th Dalai Lama Ngawang Lobsang Gyamco (for the sake of hoping him to achieve the longevity and prestige of the latter). The two High Commissioners were expected to present a memorial to the emperor signed jointly, request-ing that the confirmation could be free from the practice of drawing a lot from the golden urn to determine the soul boy, and the child should be directly confirmed as the Dalai Lamaís soul boy. On account of the consensus reached by the Regent and Tibetan monks and lay people on the memorial, which was presented through the High Commissioners, together with the fact that Emperor Jiaqing had been in power for a comparatively short period, the confirmation of the soul boy was even-tually authorized in January 1808. Emperor Jiaqing promulgated that "the boy could recite the scriptures since childhood and was able to discern the image and belongings of Buddha. I assuredly confirm him as Dalai Lama's soul boy."

In the ninth lunar month of the same year, the sitting-in-the-bed ceremony for the enthronement of the 9th Dalai Lama was held in the Potala Palace. The central government sent an envoy to Lhasa to attend the ceremony. After checking the memorial presented by Tibetan monks and lay people through the High Commissioners, the Emperor approved the determination of the soul boy could be exempt from drawing a lot from the golden urn. In order to express gratitude for the Emperorís grace, on the second day of the enthronement ceremony for the 9th Dalai Lama, leading Tibetan monks and lay people, along with the High Commissioners, made a special visit to the Potala Palace, where the practice of drawing a lot from the golden urn would originally have been carried out. They presented offerings as their thankfulness before the memorial tablets and images of the deceased emperors.

However, the 9th Dalai Lama died in 1815 at the age of 11, during which period some great events occurred in Tibet.

One was that in October 1811, Indian Viceroy Mingtog sent Manning to Tibet to worship the 9th Dalai Lama Lungtog Gyamco. Based on *History of British Invasion of Tibet* by Younghusband, on December 17, 1811, Manning was bound for the Potala Palace to be received by the Dalai Lama. Upon arriving at the mansion, he made formal greeting by kowtowing three times to the Dalai Lama and once to the Regent. Then, he sat on the cushion near Dalai Lama, demonstrating that British colonialism was conspiring to extend into Tibet and contact Tibetan political and religious leaders.

Another event was in 1814, the Tibetan Year of Wooden Dog, when the registration of Living Buddhas in Tibet, the Kham area and Inner Mongolia was completed. The register in Tibetan was re-collated in comparison with the one in Chinese. There were 167 living Buddhas in the register, including 33 in Han and Mongolian areas and 134 in Tibet and Amdo Kham area, with their names, birth place, birth year and age. The practice of drawing a lot from the golden urn could not be adopted to all the living Buddhas. The feasible approach by the imperial court to administer some of the issues on Living Buddhasí soul boys, and the registration, made it easier for the golden urn practice.

X. The Search and Confirmation of the 10th Dalai Lama

After the death of the 9th Dalai Lama Lungtog Gyamco, Emperor Jiaqing nominated Dimo Hotogtu Dianbei Gungbo as Regent, and gave orders to search for the soul boy. With the approval of the Qing court, Regent Living Buddha Dimo sent people out searching. In December 1818, Lobsang Nyiangzha's son born in Litang in May 1816 was found. Galoons and abbots of major monasteries congregated that year-end and called for the affirmation without lot drawing as exercised with the 9th Dalai Lama. Such could be seen in the *Biography of the 10th Dalai Lama,* by Abbot Darkhan Lobsang, which said:that the soul boy found in Litang turned out to be very intelligent. Parties concerned in consent requested to follow the practice with 9th Dalai Lama (in 1807), without a lot-drawing ceremony giving affirmation to the soul boy as the Dalai Lama and meanwhile approve his enthronement ceremony in order to save time.

However, Regent Dimo Hotogtu fell ill and died in march 1819 before the arrival of court approval. In that case, to determine the nominee for Regent became urgent. Living Buddha Ceimoling's soul boy Ngawang Gyainbei Curchen Gyamco took on the responsibilities of Regent.

Emperor Jiaqing believed that the 9th Dalai lived only for 11 years, and the soul boy might not be as intelligent as had been reported in order to get exemption. A lot-drawing ceremony was necessary, therefore, and he issued an edict ordering that three soul boy candidates be found and the lot-drawing ceremony held.

With this, Chemoiling Normenkhan sent circulars to headmen of the Xigaze area, Ngari, northern Tibet, Gyiar, Darbu, Dorgansi, Dorsima advising them to search and report all intelligent children. It turned out that one in Gongbo, one in Renbo Zong, and one in Gyiade Garu, one in Qamdo, and one in Qamdo Sagang were suitable. Based on these reports, specialists were sent for further investigation. On their return, Panchen Dainbai

Nyima was invited to determine who could be more intelligent besides the one from Litang, and he nominated the two from Qamdo. All headmen were convened at the Potala Palaceís Sengqoin Kangsum Hall in 1821, to hear the whole story of the search for the Dalai Lama soul boy, and ask for advice as what to do. They all agreed that the other two from Qamdo besides the one from Litang conformed with the guidance from the deities and should be reported to the emperor for the lot-drawing ceremony. Chemoiling Normenkhan wrote to the High Commissioners in this vein. The Panchen Erdeni also submitted a written agreement with his seal, and the two High Commissioners sent out the report to Emperor on July 29, 1821.

It happened that Emperor Jiaqing died before long, but his successor Emperor Daoguang approved the report. The lot-drawing ceremony was held in the Sasum Namgyi Hall of the Potala Palace on January 15, 1822. As described in the *Biography of the 10th Dalai Lama*: "At sunrise, the

Tibetan officials presenting Mandala as gift to the 14th Dalai Lama in the Potala Palace.
CHEN ZONTGLIE

Panchen went to Potala Palace from Norbu Lingka, where all officials sat in front of the portrait of Emperor, and the two High Commissioners also arrived before long. With all the officials and monks present, a Manchu amanuensis wrote the names of the three boys in Manchu rian on one side of three lots respectively, and a Tibetan amanuensis wrote on the other side in Tibetan respectively, and they checked it together, and then put the lots in the golden urn, which was shaken and one lot drawn. Since the result turned out to be in line with people's wishes, all were happy with it.

This was the first time to determine the soul boy of Dalai Lama by lot-drawing ceremony. The High Commissioners and other officials seemed to have done a lot for the preparation. When the lot-drawing result was declared, the High Commissioners gave the soul boy a writ in Mandarin, Manchu, Tibetan and Mongolian languages through Regent Chemoiling Normenkhan, telling him not to forget the good ties between the Emperor and his predecessor as Dalai Lamas and study hard to return the imperial benevolence.

The result of lot-drawing was reported to the Emperor for approval and for selecting an auspicious date for the sitting-in-the-bed ceremony. Meanwhile, preparation for this started in Tibet. The emperorís reply was announced to the soul boy by the two High Commissioners. Therefore, in April, the 7th Panchen and Regent Normenkhan, the two High Commissioners and other officials and eminent monks went to Dewagyian Monastery in Nytang Rewadui. As they arrived in the Grand Sutra Hall, the soul boy worshiped on bended knees to the east on a cushion, and Zongye Yukang Gyainbei Deleg read out the imperial edict "The chosen lot bears the name of the son of the Tibetan named Lobsang Nyiangzha who has appeared outstandingly intelligent through our investigation and is truly the soul boy of Dalai Lama.... Vouchsafe the soul boy presents including a *hada* scarf, a portrait of Buddha and a string of beads. Also grant Panchen Erdeni, Ngawang Gyainbei Curchen Gyamco each with a hada scarf and a portrait of Buddha. The Dalai Lama sitting-in-the-bed ceremony for the enthronement of the Dalai Lama will be held on August 8. I will send Wengang, Chengdu General Suchongnga, Zanggyia Hotogtu to attend. Zanggyia Hotogtu will go from Beijing. Since Panchen Erdeni has tonsured and given instructions to Dalai Lama, as there will be some months before the sitting-in-the-bed ceremony, [the soul boy] could go back home in the Xigaze area during this period. Sitting-in-the-bed related affairs be taken care of by Wengang, Baochang, Suchongnga. ..... Dalai Lama, Panchen, and those Hotogtus and other peers fell down to thank Emperoris kindness.i

Lamas with the Gandain Monastery performing Buddhist rituals. **CHEN ZONTGLIE**

In the *Biography of the 10th Dalai Lama*, regarding the granting of the golden seal of authority to the Dalai Lama, it says for the late Dalai Lama, the golden seal of his authority was in use from his sitting-in-the-bed ceremony, for this soul boy, the golden seal should be allowed to be used after his sitting-in-the-bed. Following precedent, Zanggyian Hotogtu, appointed by the emperor, went to Nytang on July 14 that year to deliver the imperial decree, and give presents to the soul boy's father Lobsang Nyiangzha.

As for the sitting-in-the-bed ceremony for the 10th Dalai Lama, according to Tibetan historical materials: "That day, Dalai Lama rode happily on late Dalai Lama's horse with a name as Yangcha Zholgar.... The Dalai Lama greeted the imperial envoy and the High Commissioners, and other non-Tibetan officials, who then left after tea. Blessing people who came to worship him, the Dalai went on to Sasum Namgyi Residence to salute the emperor's portrait. He went along and on his way to the Grand Sutra Hall in the Potala Palace, he presented *hada* scarves to the holy stupa of the 5th Dalai Lama and prayed. In the Grand Sutra Hall of Potala Palace, Zanggyia Hotogtu, Suchongnga and the two High Commissioners gathered, and they sat down and presented the Dalai Lama with the treasures on the table that the emperor gave him together with other presents. The Dalai accepted these and knelt down facing east. Regent Normenkhan, sutra teacher Living Buddha Cheqoiling, Galoon officials all knelt, too. Then, the emperor's decree on the Dalai Lama's investiture was issued and read out by Zongye abbot Yukawa: "According to the two High Commissioners' report, since you, the soul boy was born, you could recognize Buddha that predecessor Dalai Lama laid offerings for, and the stuffs he used.... After the Hotogtus prayed for seven days and Panchen Erdeni prayed, your name was taken out from the golden urn. I made this decree to appoint you as the soul boy of the Dalai Lama, and to send High Commissioner Wengang, Chengdu General Suchongnga, Zanggyia Hotogtu on the eighth day of the eighth lunar month of the year to the Potala Palace together to arrange for your sitting-in-the-bed..."

After this, people routinely worshiped on bended knees, and the High Commissioners and imperial envoy presented hada scarves to Dalai Lama. Officials took cushions and clothes granted by the emperor to the Dalai Lama. He took out a monk's cap and cloak and put them on, which well fitted him. After such court-related rites, so came the solemn Tibetan ceremony.

In 1824, to determine the soul boy of Living Buddha Razheng, a lot-drawing ceremony was held. The Dalai Lama, the two High Commissioners and other officials and monks were present before the portrait of the emperor in Sasum Namgyi of the Potala Palace, and confirmed that the boy born in Ozhub was Living Buddha Razheng's soul boy. On April 13, to determine the soul boy of Living Buddha Dimo, another lot-drawing ceremony was held, and the boy born in Qamdo was confirmed. According to the *Biography of the 10th Dalai Lama*, in 1831, the Sasum Namgyi Residence in the southern part of the Red Palace of the Potala Palace needed renovation, and the portrait of the emperor should be moved to Sengqoin Qamkang. The two High Commissioners came, they and Dalai Lama at Sasum Namgyi Residence presented *hada* scarves and exchanged greetings. Amid music, the Dalai Lama, the two High Commissioners, Regent Normenkhan worshiped the emperor's portrait, and Galoon officials Xazha took the portrait and Galoon official Tungba held emperorís name tablet, following 20 lamas with the Namgyi Zhacang leading the parade on the left, and officials and peers leading the parade on the right. With a second round of music, the portrait and name tablet was placed in Sengqoin Qamkang. Then, to accompaniment of the third round of music, the Dalai Lama presented *hada* scarves and worshiped the portrait, and 10 monks of Namgyi Zhacang performed rites for it. In October of that year, with similar rituals the portrait and tablet were moved back to their former places in the Sasum Namgyi Residence.

In 1834, the 7th Panchen Dainyima took the position of abbot, and before a statue of Sakyamuni in the new Grand Sutra Hall of the Potala Palace, he conducted bhiksu rituals for the 10th Dalai Lama. Emperor Daoguang issued a decree and granted presents to them.

After the confirmation of the 10th Dalai Lama, the Gaxag government granted his parents a manor and serfs in Nyimo County, and his family became members of the peerage. Later, probably a relative of the 10th Dalai Lama allied with Yutog, and the two families combined as the Sub-Yutog Clan.

Golden top of the Jokhang Monastery.
CHEN ZONTGLIE

XI. The Confirmation of the 11th and 12th Dalai Lamas

In September 1837, the 10th Dalai Lama died. After the administration of Regent Living Buddha Ceimoling, the augury of the living Buddhas including the 7th Panchenm Erdeni, and the consultation of High Commissioners, Regent and abbots from the three major monasteries, the Zhaibung Monastery abbot Lobzui Dainba and Sengga Sanggyi Besang with the Potala Palace were sent east resulting in confirming of four intelligent children as soul boy candidates, including one found in Shannan, one found in Gongbo and two in Sichuan. The High Commissioners reported to Emperor Daoguang in December 1840, requesting that the boys be sanctioned to proceed with a lot-drawing ceremony. Following imperial approval, the four soul boy candidates and their family members were received in Deqen Sang'aka Monastery, located in Darze County near Lhasa. The four were first investigated by the 7th Panchen Erdeni, the High Commissioners, the Regent, abbots from the three major monasteries and Galoon officials, requiring them to identify relics of the late Dalai Lama, which resulted in the consensus that all were intelligent. Hence, the High Commissioners presented their memorial to the Emperor for the lot-drawing ceremony. In May 1841, the ceremony was held in Potala Palace, selecting the boy from Taining in the Kham area, and High Commissioners noted down in a memorial the overall process. After this, the Panchen tonsured the soul boy and named him Kezhub Gyamco. In the meantime, High Commissioner Mengbao wrote another memorial, requesting the Emperor's approval for the sitting-in-the-bed ceremony, April 16 being considered an auspicious day.

After Emperor Daoguang's sanction, the central court dispatched Shimoiníe in Chengdu and the 5th Zanggyia Hotogtu to Tibet for inspecting the 11th Dalai Lamaís sitting-in-the-bed ceremony with a total sum of 10,000 taels of silver bestowed by the Emperor for expenditure. On April

16, 1842, the High Commissioners and Regent received the soul boy into the Potala Palace, where rows of monks welcomed them along with the imperial envoys and Living Buddha Zanggyia. The Regent and Galoon officials carried the imperial decree amid incense into the Sixi Puncog Hall. The soul boy worshipped to the east on bended knees on a cushion, accepted the golden sheets of confirmation and golden seal of authority awarded by the Emperor, reverently listened to the decree, and exchanged *hada* scarves with the High Commissioners. Then, the soul boy stepped onto the throne to receive *hada* scarves from Regent Living Buddha Ceimoling and Living Buddha Zanggyia and the offerings from monks and people of all circles, accompanied by instrumental music.

After the 11th Dalai Lama's sitting-in-the-bed ceremony, on July 1844, the High Commissioners reported to Emperor Daoguang on the corruption of Regent, which resulted from the estrangement between the High Commissioners and Regent Chemoiling Normenkhan Ngawang Gyiangbao Curchen Gyamco. Accordingly, he was deposed by Emperor Daoguang after 25 years in the postition. Besides, his mansion in Lhasa and all the 144, 000 taels of silver he held were sequestrated and respectively awarded to the monasteries in the Xigaze area as monk pensions, and his 278 hectoliters of rice and 6,946 hectoliters of wheat, beans and *qingke* barley were distributed to officials and soldiers in the Xigaze area. After having been imprisoned by Qishang, Living Buddha Ceimoling's fellow monks in

Statue of the 11th Dalai Lama (1838-1855) preserved in the Potala Palace.
CHEN ZONTGLIE

the Sera Monastery rescued him and settled him in the Sera Monastery. The matter was peacefully resolved by the 7th Panchen's intercession with some monks being penalized. Living Buddha Ceimoling was handed over by Sera Monastery and sent to Heilongjiang by Emperor Daoguang (in fact, he returned to his hometown of Zhonyi in Gansu, where he passed away after a couple of years. Later, his soul boy was restored in virtue at the request of the chief of the Turhu Tribe in Xinjiang). In view of the malpractice resulting from the Regent holding sole power for a long time, Qishang created a new 29-article ordinance, in which he specifically prescribed the authority, position and regulations of the Regent. After the removal of Regent Living Buddha Ceimoling, Qishang proposed to make the 7th Panchen Erdeni Dainbei Nyima the Regent. The 63-year-old Panchen turned this down on the grounds that no previous Panchen Erdeni had ever held the postition of Regent and he would inevitably become entangle in the dissensions of the top monks in Lhasa. He didn't accept the offer until August 1844 after High Commissioner Qishangís persuasion and the Emperor's approval. Upon reaching Lhasa, the Panchen Erdeni headed for the Hall of Potala Palace, performing the rogation ceremony in front of the tablet and image of the Emperor. When the Panchen interviewed the Dalai Lama in the Potala Palace, he expressed he wish of returning to the Xigaze area soon because of his senility. In March of the same year, after being Regent for no more than seven months, the 7th Panchen persisted in abdicating the position and returned to the Tashilhungpo monastery, to be replaced by Living Buddha Razheng. On the occasion of handing over as Regent, the *Biography of the 11th Dalai Lama* recorded that "on the 26th day of the fourth lunar month in 1845, the Emperor ordained Razheng Ngachitu Normenkha to take charge of Tibetan issues. The Panchen and Regent started from Norbu Lingka to go to the Potala Palace with the seal of authority, and Razheng Ngachitu departed from Jokhang Monastery at sunrise, passed through Puncog

Duilang at the gate of the Potala Palace, and went into the eastward bedroom to step onto the Regentís throne. The Palace kitchen immediately served tea and food. Afterwards, Living Buddha Razheng went to the Dorchi chamber in Sengqoin Puncog to meet the Dalai Lama and the Panchen, presenting *hada* scarves to them both. After drinking the tea offered by the Dalai Lama and the Panchen, Living Buddha Razheng entered the Sunlight Hall, where the Dalai Lama and the Panchen handed over the Regentís seal of authority. Living Buddha Razheng then bowed on bended knees and presented Mandala and the image of Buddha before retuning to his seat to accept offerings from the local governments in Tibet." At the beginning of 1846, when the 11th Dalai Lama was nine, he acknowledged the 7th Panchen as his master, and was initiated as a Buddhist novice before Sakyamuni's image in the Jokhang Monastery.

At the beginning of 1855, the 11th Dalai Lama came to power following Emperor Xiangfeng's order, and Razheng Hotogtu was in charge of business matters. The Gaxag government held a grand celebration for the Dalai Lama coming to power, which was described in the *Biography of the 11th Dalai Lama.*

Nevertheless, the 18-year-old 11th Dalai Lama Kezhub Gyamco abruptly passed away in Potala Palace on December 15 after less than a year in power. Emperor Xiangfeng appointed Razheng Hotogtu as interim Regent.

After the confirmation of the 11th Dalai Lama, the Tibetan local government transferred the manor in Gyanglho of Gyangze as the property of his father's family, who were called Puncog Kangsa for they possessed a manor in Lhasa, thus being entitled iRaoxi Punkangbaî, or Punkang Family.

Emperor Xiangfeng installed Living Buddha Razheng as Regent after the 11th Dalai Lama's demise at the end of 1855. After that, the Regent issued proclamations to U-Tsang, Darbu, Gongbo, Ngari, northern Tibet and Kham area, requesting them to report on intelligent children born in recent years, and three boys from Sangri, Oika and Darbu Lhasoi were viewed as showing inherent auspices. Soon after, the page servant of Dalai Lama of the previous generation—abbot Gomang Geshi Ngawang Norbu and Maizhacang Gongbo Geshi Ngawang Curchen with the Sera Monastery— were sent to the birthplaces of the three boys for inspection, from which the boy born in Oika was believed to be more intelligent than the other two. Details about the three boys and the descriptions of their parents, relatives and neighbors were all reported to Regent Living Buddha Razheng. After the consultation among the Regent, Galoon officials and Jichiao abbot, sutra teacher Lobsang Qenrao Wangqug (Living Buddha Dezhub), Qoizang Yishi Gyamco and Living Buddha Bebo were invited to give auguries. Also, the three Buddhist Guardian, including Lhamo Buddhist Guardian and Samye Buddhist Guardian, were asked for instruction, and they unanimously suggested a lot-drawing ceremony. Then, the abbots from all monasteries, headed by three major ones of Sera, Zhaibung and Gandain, diaconal monks and officials at all levels in local governments were convened to attend a conference. The Regent gave an introduction about the search and inspection of each intelligent boy and the replies they got from the auguries and deities, which resulted in the decision that the ilot-drawing ceremony is necessary for confirmationî. In line with what was written in *Biography of the 12th Dalai Lama,* before the lot-drawing ceremony, procedures in seeking soul boy needed to be carried out step by step with the consultations of monks, lay officials and the High Commissioners. With the Emperor's authorization, "they (referring to the three boysî family members and masters) were received in Galsang Phodrang Palace of Norbu Lingka. In the place where major officials and Living Buddhas usually assembled, the images, daily articles and strings of beads with fake ones were displayed to the boys for selection. Only the intelligent boy born in Oika unerringly distinguished all the articles belonging to the late Dalai Lama. On the 13th day, Razheng Hotogtu, the High Commissioners and other Han and Tibetan officials got together in the Sunlight Hall of Norbu Lingka Galsang Phodrang Palace to interview the three intelligent boys. Impressed by their excellent appearance, the High commissioners felt satisfied after their personal inspection, and soon asked the Emperor for a lot-drawing with the three boys' names placed in golden urn." After the Emperor's sanction, on the second day of the first lunar month of 1858, the golden urn was transferred from the Jokhang Monastery of Lhasa to the Sasum Namgyi Hall in the Potala Palace, where the Emperor's portrait was displayed. For the next 11 days, eminent monks including sutra teacher Living Buddha Purbojor and monks and laymen from Namgyi Zhacang read scriptures in front of the golden urn. On the 13th day of the month, the two High Commissioners and Razheng Hotogtu attended the ceremony. After the secretary put the intelligent boysí names in the language of the Manchurian ethnic group on one side of each lot and Kamzhong in Tibetan language on the other side, all the lots were handed over to Regent and the High Commissioners for examination in case of error. The High Commissioners subsequently kowtowed in front of the Emperor's portrait, and placed the lots into the golden urn. All the attendees began reading scriptures in chorus, and the High Commissioners performed the ceremonial ritual by kowtowing to the Emperorís portrait before shaking the golden urn. The lot that fell from it was checked by the Hotogtu and the High Commissioners, and afterward, the name of Oika Lobsang Dainzin Jumai was read out. People on the spot burst into a hail of, "Lhagyialho" (the Deity won). The High Commissioners turned to the soul boyís father, Puncog Cewang, saying, "Your son Lobsang Dainzin Jumai has been confirmed as the Dalai Lama's soul boy by the lot-drawing ceremony, and you should kowtow to appreciate the Emperor's benefaction", which Puncog Cewang did and then presented *hada* scarves to the High Commissioners and the Hotogtu.

After lot-drawing ceremony, Razheng Hotogtu dispatched Galoon official Xazha Wangqug Gyibo instantly to Gongsa Richu—the soul boy's birthplace—to announce the final result, and the soul boy was received at Galsang Phodrang Palace in Norbu Lingka to live. On the 15th day of the month, Regent Razheng Hotogtu tonsured the soul boy and granted him the name Ngawang Lobsang Dainbei Gyaincain Chilai Gyamco (usually called Chilai Gyamco). Soon the Emperor's decree arrived, in which the soul boy was formally confirmed. The Emperor bestowed the edict and gifts on the soul boy that were handed over by the High Commissioners and the Regent on the 15th day of the fourth lunar month. On that day, monks with the Sera Monastery, the Zhaibung Monastery, the Moru Monastery, four lings, the Gyibori and Namgyi Zhacang lined up between the government office of the High Commissioners in Maigyi and the Norbu Lingka. Galoon officials, Zhasake and other delegates reverently welcomed the edict as it passed. The Dalai Lama's soul boy reached Lhunzhub Garcha Hall in the Norbu Lingka just at the time when the edict was brought up. It was immediately placed on the table and then placed in the Hall upon the High Commissionersí arrival. Top officials above Phoboin and Depoin from the local government, headed by Razheng Hotogtu, knelt facing east, and listened to Zongye abbot reading the edict, after which all the people knelt down three times and kowtowed nine times, followed by the presenting of *hada* scarves for the soul boy. It was recorded in *Biography of the 12th Dalai Lama* that, "on the seventh day of the ninth lunar month, the Emperor conferred a title of Duke upon Dalai Lamaís father, along with an official hat."

Biography of the 12th Dalai Lama recorded the sitting-in-the-bed for the 12th Dalai Lama held in 1860 in the Potala Palace as follows: High Commissioners arrived with the Emperor's edict at the time, Dalai Lama and Regent Hotogtu were kneeling down on the cushions toward the east, and so were Galoon officials. Right after Manchurian Zongye and Kamzhong finished reading in the Manchurian and Tibetan language the Emperor's edict that was awarded to the Dalai Lama and Regent Hotogtu, those present including the Dalai Lama and Regent knelt down three times and kowtowed nine times. With that, the High Commissioners offered gifts and *hada* scarves to the Dalai Lama and Regent, who presented *hada* scarves in return.

It was just the time when the Opium War broke out. At the last stage of Qing Regime, envoys were dispatched with the mission of commanding the High Commissioners to survey the sitting-in-the-bed ceremony for the 12ᵗʰ Dalai Lama.

The year of 1853 saw the death of the 7ᵗʰ Panchen Dainbei Nyima at the age of 70. The 8ᵗʰ Panchen Erdeni was not able to participate in the confirmation and sitting-in-the-bed ceremony of the 12ᵗʰ Dalai Lama due to his youth.

Shortly after this ceremony, a severe conflict within the Tibetan governing group broke out. In 1862, Regent Razheng Hotogtu collided with the monks from Zhaibung Monastery, which originated from an abbotís dismissal for docking donations by Regent Hotogtu. Unhappy with the disposal, monks and laymen with the Zhaibung Monastery incited a disturbance. High Commissioner Manqing sent commissioner Li Yupu in charge of food supplies and partisan Tang Huaiwu with Han troops to suppress the troublem but Li's partiality towards the Zhaibung Monastery exacerbated the situation. Furthermore, monks there contacted lamas with the Gandain Monastery, took cannon from the armory of the Potala Palace and fired toward the Regentís residence.

On the one hand, Razheng reported the event to the High Commissioners, and on the other hand, he organized people to retaliate by shooting back. Being outnumbered, Razheng had no choice but to flee during the night with the Regent's official seal after only one day's fighting. According to Ya Hanzhang's record in *Biography of the 12th Dalai Lama,* "After Razheng Hotogtu left Lhasa, he was bound for Beijing though Qinghai to make an accusation to the central government. Appointed as the investigator, Foji set out for Tibet, but failed due to bad roads. Li Yupu was asked to go up to Beijing for questioning, but was shielded by High Commissioners. The case eventually ended in nothing with Razhengís death in Beijing."

Biography of the 12th Dalai Lama recorded this conflict within the leadership as follows: In 1862, the discordance among Regent Razheng Hotogtu, Gandain and delegates with the Zhaibung Monastery bred a tremendous turmoil. Though Daqen with the Sagya Sect and the delegates with the Tashilhungpo Monastery made great efforts in mediation, things remained unsettled on the 12th day of the third lunar month, the Dalai Lama accepted the edict and began taking charge of political affairs".

This made it clear that when no political and religious leader could be accredited, Dalai Lama was able to wield power in name with the edict and golden seal of authority bestowed to the successive Dalai Lamas.

Although the relieved Galoon official Xazha Wangqug Gyibo took charge of political issues, it differed from the cases of previous living Buddhas acting as Regent. It was unprecedented for the Qing regime to warrant a layperson as a political official, not a formal Regent, to assist the Dalai Lama under special circumstances.

In 1864, following the previous routines, the 12th Dalai Lama was granted the full status of a monk by his sutra teacher tonsured and relieved Gandan Chiba Abbot Dezhub Lobsang Qenrao Wangqug before the figurine of a reclining Buddha in the Jokhang Monastery in Lhasa. On the 25th day of the eighth Tibetan month that year, Dixi Normenkhan Xazha Wangqug Gyibo died of sickness in Lhunzhub Garcha Hall of Norbu Lingka, after being in the power for two years. On the 29th day of the month, the Dalai Lama instructed sutra teacher Dezhub Qenrao

Golden sheets of confirmation Qing Emperor Xianfeng bestowed to the 11th Dalai Lama.   CHEN ZONTGLIE

Wangqug to assume political and religious duties, and report the relevant issues to the High Commissioners and the Emperor.

Afterward, the Regent came to Sunlight Hall offering *hada* scarves and gifts to the Dalai Lama, and ascended to the Regentís throne. Because the Dalai Lama was not yet nine, and the war continued, Dezhub was instated as Regent in advance with a simple ceremony by the High Commissioners, for fear of a vacuum in political affairs.

In 1865, Regent Gandan Chiba Abbot was entitled Normenkhan and ordered to assist in the sending out of political edicts. In accordance with conventions, the High Commissioners delivered the edict to the Sunlight Hall at sunrise. The Dalai Lama, Regent and Hotogtu devoutly knelt down and listened to the Emperorís edict. It was obvious that Living Buddha Dezhub attained the title of Regent Normenkhan from the Qing government after taking up the post of Regent.

Regent Living Buddha Dezhub passed away in 1873. According to the Emperor's decree, the 12th Dalai Lama came to power in 1874, and a

ceremonious celebration was held. In the next year, however, the 12th Dalai Lama died in the Potala Palace.

The 12th Dalai Lama's father also received lots of manors and serfs. Later, the family combined with the manors of Lhalu Garchawa of the 8th Dalai Lama to form the Rao Lhalu clan whose territory exceeded all other aristocrats.

∧
∧ *Golden seal of authority qing Emperor Xianfeng bestowed to the 11th Dalai Lama.*
CHEN ZONTGLIE

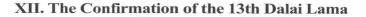

XII. The Confirmation of the 13th Dalai Lama

In the third lunar month of 1875, the 12th Dalai Lama died. The monks and common people in Tibet publicly recommended Jilung Hutogtu as the Regent and asked the High Commissioners to report to the Court accordingly. In 1877, Emperor Guangxu granted the name of Tongshang to the Regent. From then on, Dagch Jilung Hutogtu served as Regent formally with the name of Tongshang Hutogtu. At the same time, the Regent charged the Tibetan Gaxag government with the task of sending people to find the soul boy of Dalai Lama everywhere. In 1877, the 8th Panchen Erdeni, the Regent, the three major monasteries in Lhasa, the Abbot of the Tashilhungpo Monastery, Galoon officials and other monastery and lay officials reported to the High Commissioners that they had found only one intelligent child in Gongbo after searching carefully, and all parties related recognized him as the soul boy of the Dalai Lama; they asked for exemption of the lot-drawing ceremony. The High Commissioners reported this request to Emperor Guangxu and begged for his approval. After gaining this, on 13th day of the sixth lunar month of 1879, the 13th Dalai Lama took part in the sitting-in-the-bed ceremony in the Potala Palace. There have been some passages written giving details of the search for and recognition of the 13th

Statue of the 13th Dalai (1876-1933) preserved in the Potala Palace.
CHEN ZONTGLIE

<< *The 13th Dalai Lama and his*
party on way to visit.
GYAMCO

Dalai Lama.

Biography of the 13th Dalai Lama was compiled by Regent Living Buddha Razheng Tubdain Gyiangbai Yishi Dainbei Gyaincain in 1933 after the death of the 13th Dalai Lama. At the time of writing this biography, Living Buddha Razheng was in charge of the search for the soul boy of the 13th Dalai Lama. This biography emphasized such affairs as confirming the direction of the birthplace of the soul boy, examining the reflections in Lhamo Lhaco Lake, finding out the soul boy's identity in accordance with the reflections in the lake concerning his family background, and the monks and lay people asking for the exemption of lot-drawing ceremony because they were all convinced of the true identity of the soul boy.

Not long after coming to power, the 12th Dalai Lama Chilai Gyamco died on the morning of the 20th day of the third month of 1875 in the Potala Palace with the age of 20. The Gaxag government immediately reported this to the High Commissioners. High Commissioner Xikai went to the Potala Palace at once to examine and hold the memorial ceremony. He packed and sealed the jade sheets of confirmation and jade seal of authority, golden sheets of confirmation and golden seal of authority and

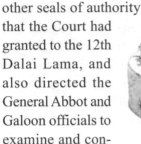

other seals of authority that the Court had granted to the 12th Dalai Lama, and also directed the General Abbot and Galoon officials to examine and con-

<<
Gifts from Empress Dowage Cixi to the 23th Dalai: Pearl Mandala.
CHEN ZONTGLIE

firm the cause of death before carrying out the funeral. After they were certain that illness was the reason, they reported to the Court on the 28th day of the fourth lunar month of 1875. In the 11th lunar month, Emperor Guangxu gave charge of Tibetan affairs to Gongdelin Ngawang Bandain, namely Living Buddha Jilung, and also with the task of searching for and recognizing the next Dalai Lama. At the request of Tibetan monks and lay people, he undertook to carry out this task urgently.

According to the Tibetan version of the *Biography of the 13th Dalai Lama,* he had died facing in a southeasterly direction in the Potala Palace.

That night, the remains were placed facing south in a cross-legged sitting pose. The next morning, the remains were found to have turned towards the southeast. Then, the body was moved to the encoffining pavilion in a sitting cross-legged posture facing south, but, one again, were found to have turned to face southeast.

According to the arrangements of Regent Living Buddha Jilung Ngawang Bandain, the

>> *Mural on wall of the Western Hal of the Potala Palace depicting how the 13th Dalai Lama payed an audience to the empress in Beijing in 1908.*
CHEN ZONTGLIE

local Tibetan Gaxag government gave a direction in the third lunar month of 1876 to the former officials and persons-in-charge in the Xigaze area and Kham area that they convey the order of searching for the soul boy of the 12th Dalai Lama and report all the newly-born children with intelligent omens. At the same time, the Gaxag government asked Neqoin and Samye Buddhist Guardian to invite the spirits of God and also asked the 8th Panchen Erdeni and other Living Buddhas to cast lots. It is said that both spirit rapping and casting lots showed that, if the soul boy of the 12th Dalai Lama were born in southeast, it would be very helpful to Tibetan Buddhism and the fate of the common people. In accordance with the divination of Neqoin Buddhist Guardian, the Tibetan local government listed all place names lying in an easterly or southeasterly direction above Dajianlu (Kangding) and assigned special persons to the search. When asking for direction from the Buddhist Guardian about who would be preferable to examine the reflections in the lake, Neqoin Buddhist Guardian indicated that the Kangsu (outgoing abbot) of Lhasa Upper Tantric School should go to Lhamo Lhaco Lake in Qoikegyi, to the southeast of Lhasa, recite sutras Ruo Song

∧ *The local government of Tibet set up the Tibet Dalai Office in Chongqing*
during the War of Resistance Against Japan. Pictured here is the office
seal and seal text.   *CHEN ZONTGLIE*

>> *Holy stupa (in the Potala Palace) that contains the remains of the 13th Dalai Lama who died in 1933.* **CHEN ZONTGLIE**

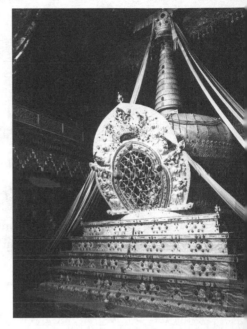

. . . .

and examine the lake reflections, and he would receive guidance.

Judui Kangsu Lobsang Dagyi went to the Lhamo Lhaco Lake from Lhasa with more than 40 attendants and acted as he had been told. According to *Biography of the 13th Dalai Lama,* it was at the end of the ninth Tibetan lunar month, and the water was abnormally clear instead of being iced over. On the surface there appeared a valley with wide span east to west, on the upper eastern side of which there were grasslands, in the northeast there was an ancient tower, in the southeast there was a square wall, with a building of 3 or 4 stories not far away. Then, he saw a village between the building and the ancient tower and many people on horseback at a corner in the south traveling east and west.

Just before the end of examination of the lake reflections, some local official in Qoikegyi told him of a family in Langdun Village, The husband was named as Gonggar Renqen and the wife was named as Lobsang Zholma, who had given birth to a boy at daybreak on the fifth day of the fifth lunar month in 1876. It was said that there was some omen before the birth of the boy. For example, on the third day of the seventh lunar month in 1875, a ghee bag had broken suddenly and the ghee flowed out, which indicated luck. In addition, in the ninth lunar month of 1875, among the pear trees before their door, there was a big one that was flourishing with flowers and all the local common people saw it. The rainbow on the roof of their house was like a tent. And the mother had also had some dream omen. Kangsu Lobsang Dagyi went to the home in Langdun to which he had been directed and saw the baby at the age of five months. When he held the infant in his arms, the baby touched Kangsu's forehead and face with his fingers. He asked the baby: "Would you like to go to Lhasa?" and the baby showed happiness. From the situation in this first meeting, this soul boy displayed many omens in accordance with those divined.

Judui Kangsu Lobsang Dagyi returned to Lhasa and reported the details of examining the reflections in the lake and the search. Everyone had felt that in order to determine the soul boy of the Dalai Lama, all Living Buddhas and the Four Buddhist Guardians should cast lots and invite the deities, in particular, Neqoin, the Buddhist Guardian, to give specific directions about the search direction, the names of parents and the scene of the birthplace. As these absolutely tallied with the real situation, it could be said the identity of the soul boy had been convincingly established. In addition, the birth date of the soul boy was a good and lucky day. The baby born in Langdun was very intelligent in accordance with the will of all monasteries and common people. The Gaxag government then assigned two close attendants, Kamqeng Qamqug Langzho and Zongye Lhawang Norbu, to check the identification. What they reported confirmed the findings of Kangsu Lobsang Dagyi.

The upper class of Tibetan monastery and common people with Regent Living Buddha Jilung Ngawang Bandain as their chief were inclined to confirm the Langdun soul boy. As the 10th, the 11th and the 12th Dalai Lama were all confirmed after lot-drawing ceremony, the soul boy in Langdun had either to be placed in such a ceremony with other two babies or be recognized as the Dalai Lama directly through exemption, like the confirmation of the 9th Dalai Lama after Court approval.

Regent Living Buddha Jilung Ngawang Bandain and other people

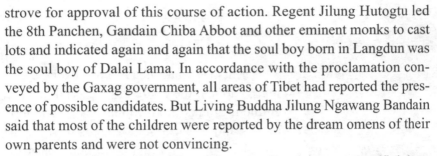

strove for approval of this course of action. Regent Jilung Hutogtu led the 8th Panchen, Gandain Chiba Abbot and other eminent monks to cast lots and indicated again and again that the soul boy born in Langdun was the soul boy of Dalai Lama. In accordance with the proclamation conveyed by the Gaxag government, all areas of Tibet had reported the presence of possible candidates. But Living Buddha Jilung Ngawang Bandain said that most of the children were reported by the dream omens of their own parents and were not convincing.

Regent Living Buddha Jilung Ngawang Bandain sent an official report to the High Commissioners, in which he described the birthplace direction, parentsí names, the results of casting lots, examining reflections in the lake, reporting, checking and other important affairs about the soul boy of the 12th Dalai Lama. He pointed out that the dream omens, auspices and other omen were all favorable. After repeated checking, all the Tibetan monks and common people recognized the soul boy born in Langdun as the soul boy of the 12th Dalai Lama, and they asked the Court to exempt him from the lot-drawing ceremony and approve his sitting-in-the-bed ceremony.

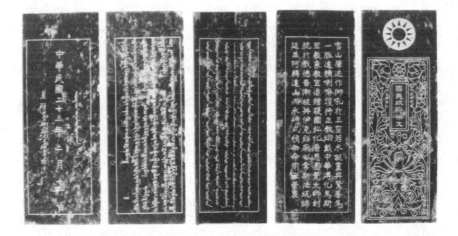

Jade sheets of confirmation the Nationalist Government bestowed to the 13th Dalai Lama.   *CHEN ZONTGLIE*

Then, Gandain Chiba Abbot led all the Living Buddhas, the leaders of the Gelug Sect, eminent monks in all monasteries, common monks and four Galoon officials to write the official report to the High Commissioners seeking such an exemption.

In order to get the High Commissioners to send this report to the Court, they paid much attention to its compilation. It first affirmed that the lot-drawing ceremony had been fixed, and then said that in the years of Jiaqing, the soul boy of the 8th Dalai Lama won the approval of the Emperor to be exempted from the lot-drawing ceremony. But the 9th Dalai Lama died at the age of 11.

Essentially, the untimely death of the 9th Dalai Lama served as the significant reason for Emperor Jiaqing to recognize the 10th Dalai Lama by the lot-drawing ceremony, so the exemption of the lot-drawing ceremony of the 9th Dalai Lama could not be the explanation for exempting that of the 13th Dalai Lama. But the official report also pointed out that, ëfrom then on, the 10th, the 11th, and the 12th Dalai Lama were all recognized by the lot-drawing ceremony according to imperial edict. But unfortunately the 10th Dalai Lama died at the age of 23, the 11th Dalai Lama died at the age of 18, and the 12th Dalai Lama died at the age of 20. This meant that, although the 9th Dalai Lama died at an untimely moment after being exempted from the lot-drawing ceremony, the three subsequent Dalai Lamas did not live long either. This cleared away an obstruction to seeking exemption of the lot-drawing ceremony of the 13th Dalai Lama. Then, after describing the life of the Dalai Lamas of various generations, it showed that the Dalai Lama before the 9th generation all lived long except the 4th and the 6th. To emphasize the tone, the official report also gave the opposition view that, neither of the other children (offered as candidates) was intelligent. If the lot-drawing ceremony was carried on, as our Tibetan people have not much fortune, it is inevitable to select some common child instead of the convincing soul boy in Darbu Langdun. Then, all monks and common people would feel it regrettable and it would be an unfavorable development. It is very clear to define the advantages and disadvantages.

In order to win approval of the exemption of the lot-drawing ceremony, the official report also pointed out a method to check the soul boy by the High Commissioners, the Panchen Erdeni and the Regent, to make it easy for Emperor to be assured, Regent Tongshang Hutogtu and other Han and Tibetan officials to be convinced, we are going to send the soul boy of Darbu Langdun to Rigyia Sangmo Dainling Monastery on the outskirts of Lhasa as soon as possible and invite the Panchen Erdeni to Lhasa. Then, the Han and Tibetan officials can order the soul boy to

recognize the Buddha Figure of the former Dalai Lama and the remains; on the other hand, the Upper Tantric School can order Lobsang Dagyi to report the fact of searching. After it is certain of being correct, the lot-drawing ceremony can be exempted, Norbu Tsang Tabok Gyimoco can be recognized as the soul boy of the 12th Dalai Lama and become the 13th Dalai Lama directly through the sitting-in-

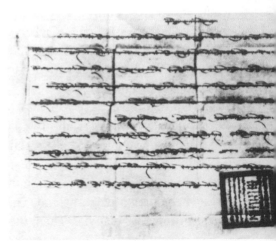

Memorial the 13th Dalai submitted to Qing Emperor Guangxu read in part: I often pray for the teachings of the Sakyamuni and the consolidation of the territory of the emperor.
CHEN ZONTGLIE

the-bed ceremony.í In fact, this procedure did exist in the recognition procedures for several former generations of Dalai Lama. The official report emphasized this only to prepare the way for the transmission of the report by the High Commissioners and the approval of the exemption of the lot-drawing ceremony by the Court. Later, this method was taken again for sitting-in-the-bed ceremony for the enthronement of the 14th Dalai Lama.

Since the Opium War in 1840, with the aggression carried out by imperialistic countries and the weakening of the power of Qing Dynasty, the Court had inclined to looseness in political and Buddhism affairs in Tibet. High Commissioners Songgui succeeded in 1876 and soon faced this significant affair of searching and recognizing the 13th Dalai Lama. After receiving the official reports from both Regent Living Buddha Jilung Ngawang Bandain and Gandain Chiba Abbot, Songgui reported to the Court on the 11th day of the fifth lunar month of 1877 and said, "What the Hutogtu had said was the fact...The original report will be sent to the military-political-affairs setup for examination."At that time, Emperor Guangxu had only just succeeded to the throne, and the power of the Court was really controlled by Empress Dowager Cixi. On the 29th of the sixth lunar month, Songgui received the imperial edict, "Norbu Tsang Tabok Gyimoco is recognized as the soul boy of Dalai Lama". This meant the Court had approved the exemption of the lot-drawing ceremony of the 13th Dalai Lama.

After winning court approval, the soul boy was welcomed to Caigungtang Monastery on the 14th day of the tenth lunar month of 1877 following the example of the 9th Dalai Lama in being exempted from the lot-drawing ceremony. In the Sunlight Hall, the soul boy sat facing east with Regent Living Buddha Jilung, the sutra teacher and other monastery and common officials behind. The High Commissioners read out the edict of Emperor Guangxu. Then, the Dalai Lama offered *hada* scarves to the east in thanks to Emperor Guangxu for his favor and asked the

High Commissioners to send them to the emperor. Monks and lay officials offered some gifts to the soul boy. On the 11th day of the first lunar month of 1878, the Regent and the Gaxag Government invited the 8th Panchen Erdeni to Caigungtang Monastery to shave the soul boyís hair and grant him the name of Gyizun Ngawang Lobsang Tubdain Gyamco Qugzha Wangqug Xoile Nambei Gyiawa Besangbo, or Tubdain Gyamco for short. On the 11th day of the first lunar month, the Dalai Lama soul boy, accompanied by the Regent, some Living Buddhas and other monastery and lay officials, set out for the Rigyia Sangdainling Monastery, north of Lhasa River, to set up residence. According to traditional rules, the soul boy could not have the formal sitting-in-the-bed ceremony until he was four years old. So, he lived for more than one year in this monastery, waiting for the confirmation of the ceremony date. In the second lunar month of 1879, Regent Living Buddha Jilung reported to the High Commissioners that the sitting-in-the-bed ceremony was going to be held on the 13th day of the sixth lunar month of 1879 and asked them to transmit this report to the emperor. After winning approval, the 13th Dalai Lama with his attendants came to the Potala Palace on the 13th day of the sixth lunar month. At first, he worshipped the statue of Emperor Qianlong on bended knees three times and knocked his head on the ground nine times, and wor-

Λ *Nationalist Government special envoy Huang Musong went to Lhasa to mourn the late 13th Dalai Lama.*   *XIN HUA*

Portrait of the 9ᵗʰ Panchen Erdeni.   *GYAMCO*

shipped other major Buddha Figures in Potala Palace. Then, he ascended to the throne of the Dalai Lama to receive the worship of monastery and lay officials. On the 14th day of the sixth lunar month, the sitting-in-the-bed ceremony was held in the Sixi Puncog Hall. From the following day, other officials of the Gaxag Government and Lhasaís three major monasteries, Living Buddhas of all monasteries and common people from everywhere came to celebrate continuously.

The Qing Dynasty still regarded the exemption of the lot-drawing ceremony for the 13th Dalai Lama as a particular case. Ten years later, in the 9th lunar month of 1887, the lot-drawing ceremony was still held before the statue of Emperor Qianlong in the Potala Palace for confirming the soul boy of the 8th Panchen Erdeni, that is the 9th Panchen Qoigyi Nyima, from among three soul boy candidates.

In 1886, Tongshang Jilung Hutogtu died. Emperor Guangxu authorized Dimo Hutogtu to succeed him as Regent. In 1895, the 13th Dalai Lama received the bhiksu ritual having made much progress in Buddhist learning. At that time, he was 20 years old. The three major monasteries and lay officials of the Gaxag government compelled Regent Dimo Hutogtu to resign with the excuse of "God's thoughts" and asked the Dalai Lama to take over power. In the eighth lunar month, he received the resignation of Regent Dimo Hutogtu and the solemn ceremony for the 13th Dalai Lama's accession to power was held in the Sixi Puncog Hall in the Potala Palace. Soon afterwards, in July 1899, the Gaxag government pretended it had been told by the Buddhist Guardian that former Regent Dimo Hutogtu Ngawang Lobsang had conspired to hide some charm in the shoes offered to the Dalai Lama. They imprisoned him and confiscated his property. Simultaneously, they incriminated Norbu Toizhub and other officials who followed the Living Buddha. Hence the 13th Dalai Lama assumed complete mastery of Tibet. This was later called the Daingyiling Event or Living Buddha Dimo Incident in history. After that, some internal conflict erupted between the 13th Dalai Lama and the 9th Panchen Erdeni followers among the upper class of Tibetan religious and lay society.

The 9th Panchen Erdeni went to Nanjing where he was received by Dai Chuanxian, a Nationalist Government official. GYAMCO

In February 1904, the British Army led by Captain Younghusband started the second war of aggression against Tibet. The brave Tibetan people made great efforts to resist. But as they were in short of the powerful support from Qing Court and their arms were so poor, they were defeated at last. On the evening of June 15th, 1904, the 13th Dalai Lama led scores of bodyguards to flee to Outer Mongolia through Tanggulha Mountain, Chadmu Basin and the Hexi Corridor. The Central Government assigned some officials to visit the Dalai Lama at once and brought some gifts to him from Emperor Guangxu and Empress Dowager Cixi. In the spring of 1906, the 13th Dalai Lama started back to Tibet. On April 25th, Emperor Guangxu and Empress Dowager Cixi sent the imperial envoy Guo Zuo, the Minister in Charge of Religious Affairs in Mongolia and Tibet, and other officials to visit the Dalai Lama. The latter arrived in Xining and moved to the Tar

<< *Golden Buddha lantern used by Huang Musong to mourn the late 13th Dalai Lama. CHEN ZONGLIE*

Monastery in Qinghai. On November 29, 1907, he started off from the Tar Monastery to travel to Beijing according to the imperial edict. He lived in Wutai Mountain at first. On July 27, 1908, the Qing Court sent an envoy to Wutai Mountain to ask the Dalai Lama to start off to Beijing for a meeting with Emperor, and he arrived in the capital on the third day of the eighth lunar month finally. On the 20th day, the 13th Dalai Lama went to court and met with Empress Dowager Cixi and Emperor Guangxu. Two months later, Empress Dowager Cixi and Emperor Guangxu died. Then, the 13th Dalai Lama started back to Tibet in the 11th lunar month of 1908.

When he arrived in Tibet in 1909, the Qing Court was conducting reform in the Kham area and had sent the Sichuan army to Tibet, which threatened the political and economic interests of the upper classes in Tibet, leading to conflict. As a result, the 13th Dalai Lama changed his intention of resisting the British army stoutly to protecting his own political power and interests with British support. Before arriving in Tibet, the 13th Dalai Lama directed Lhunqen Xazha Banjor Dorje to assemble the Tibetan army and peopleís militia to hold back the Sichuan army. He even invited the British minister to compel the Qing Court to stop the Sichuanese from entering Tibet. In the 11th lunar month of 1909, the 13th Dalai Lama returned to Lhasa. He assigned Xazha Banjor Dorje and two other pro-British aristocrats as Lhunqen in charge of administration. In the second lunar month of 1910, the Sichuan army led by Zhongying arrived in Lhasa and began fighting sporadically with the Tibetan army immediately. The 13th Dalai Lama, who had had a frosty relationship with High Commissioners Lianyu, felt more restless. He assigned Living Buddha Ceimoling as Regent and ordered him to stay in Lhasa, while he himself led Lhunqen Xazha and some officials to flee. Lianyu sent some sent soldiers in pursuit, but they were attacked by Tibetans in Quxhui and could not catch the fleeing party. At the end of the second lunar month, the 13th Dalai Lama arrived in Darjeeling, India, through Yadong. Based on the report from High Commissioners Lianyu, the Qing Court abolished the title of the 13th Dalai Lama while Britain welcomed him warmly, and made preparations for him to visit various parts of India and provided him with lodging and articles for daily use. They permitted the Dalai Lama to establish an exiled Gaxag Government in Darjeeling. He kept in contact with the officials of Tibetan local government in Lhasa, controlled the situation in Tibet and made preparations for invasion.

<A shot of the Gyangze Resisting-British-Invasion Memorial Hall.>
LI MIAN

On October 10, 1911, revolution broke out in China. The Qing Dynasty was overthrown and the feudal system lasting for over 2,000 years came to an end. The Republic of China (1912-1949) was established. On January 1, 1912, Sun Yat-sen became the temporary president based in Nanjing. In his inaugural address, he emphasized that, "a country is founded on people. National unity means the unity of Han, Manchu, Mongolian, Hui and Tibetan areas and the unity of Han, Manchu, Mongolian, Hui and Tibetan people." In March, Sun took charge of establishing and publicizing The Provisional Constitution of the Republic of China, which served as the temporary constitution. In it, it is written that "the Republic of China covers 12 provinces, Inner and Outer Mongolia, Tibet and Qinghai." It also stipulated that, as to the senators of the Nationalist Government, Tibet could select five delegates, equal to those of other provinces and Inner and Outer Mongolia. The selection procedure was decided by the local government. In April, Yuan Shi-kai succeeded to the position of president. In his presidential order, he declared that "the area of Mongolia, Tibet and Hui belongs to the territory of the Republic of China, and the people of Mongolia, Tibet and Hui are the people of the Republic of China." He established the Bureau in Charge of the Mongolian and Tibetan Affairs. Since then, in the constitution of the Republic of China, it had been clearly recorded that Tibet belonged to China and was part of Chinese territory. In October, the 13th Dalai Lama wrote from India to bureau director Gungsang Norbu: "I am willing to maintain Buddhism and please transfer my intention for proper discussion." Yuan Shi-kai then ordered the restoration of the title of Dalai Lama, but an attempt by an official based in India to confer the title was blocked by the British.

After the Revolution of 1911, British imperialism made use of the chaos in Tibet to make mischief. The British Indian Viceroy went to Darjeeling immediately to have discussions with the Dalai Lama. He provided the Dalai Lama with arms and money, the latter, in turn, sent some of his favorites including Dasang Zhamdong to return to Tibet. They assembled a several thousand-strong peopleís militia to attack the Sichuan army in Lhasa, Xigaze, Gyangze and other regions. The Dalai Lama ordered all Tibetan monasteries and common people to break off relations with the Han government and to cut off the provision for the Sichuan army and Han officials in Tibet. In the summer of 1912, Sichuan

>> Sculpture of the 13th Dalai in the Potala Palace. CHEN ZONTGLIE

and Yunnan sent some forces to support the Sichuan army in Tibet and even occupied Gyangda. But because of the intervention and the pressure from Britain, Yuan Shi-kai had to order Sichuan and Yunnan to halt this support. After the Revolution of 1911, the Sichuan army had been divided into several groups. Because of the continuous fighting among themselves and the shortage of support, they gradually came to the end with no arms and provisions. Later, the Nepalese delegate in Lhasa served as a coordinator to hold negotiation on a ceasefire between Zhongying and Lhunqen Qamqenpa assigned by the Dalai Lama. The Sichuan army gave up its arms before returning to the hinterland through Gyangze, Yadong and India under the protection of Nepal and British officials. By the end of December 1912, Lianyu, Zhongying and other officials and the Sichuan army had all left Tibet. The 13th Dalai Lama returned to Lhasa in the middle of December 1912 and punished the monks of Daingyiling Monastery who had followed Living Buddha Dimo and supported the High Commissioners and the Sichuan army. Some monasteries belonging to Zhaibung Monastery and aristocrats who had supported the Sichuan army were also punished. He promoted some persons credited with fighting against the Sichuan army and authorized Dasang Zhamdong as Zhasa to succeed to the post of dead pro-Han Charong Galoon officials. He also assembled the local headmen in Tibet and collected their opinions about how to manage Tibet in future. Many people especially the underclass monasteries and common people did not agree to the breaking off of contact with the central government. In addition, the army sent by Sichuan and Yunnan was in the region east of Gongbo Gyangda. As a result of various restrictions, Dalai Lama could not make decision about relations with the central government or to implement "the independence of Tibet" completely separated from China.

Although Britain had made use of various means, including the chaos in Tibet after the Revolution of 1911, to plot "the independence of Tibet", the relationship of bone and flesh between Tibet and motherland had come into being through a long history and could not be cut off by anyone. In 1919, according to the central government's direction, the Gansu provincial government assigned envoy Zhu Xiu to go to Tibet and meet with the 13th Dalai Lama. The Dalai Lama said: "I inclined towar ds Britain because of the pressure from imperial ministers instead of my own intention. Now, I am very thankful for your coming to Tibet. I hope the President can assign some full-fledged representative as soon as possible to solve this problem. I promise that I fully incline to the motherland and intend to strive for happiness of all nationalities. The Simla Conference Draft can also be modified.î In 1921, he sent some favorites including abbot Gungjor Zongnyi to Beijing to serve in the Yonghegong Lamasery. In 1929, the Kuomintang established the Nationalist Government in Nanjing and the 9th Panchen Erdeni established his branch office there. The 13th Dalai Lama then sent Gungjor Zongnyi and others to Nanjing carrying a letter to the Nationalist Government with the intention of resuming relations. The Nationalist Government asked Gungjor Zongnyi to bring the letter written by Chiang Kai-shek to Tibet and sought the Dalai Lamaís opinions on the relationship between Tibet and central government. In 1930, Gungjor Zongnyi returned to Nanjing with a reply. The Dalai Lama assigned Gungjor Zongnyi as the delegate of Tibet in Nanjing and established the branch office in Nanjing in 1931, which served as the formal organization for connecting Tibet and the central government.

In 1931, the Nationalist Government held a conference in Nanjing for framing a new constitution and invited the delegates from Tibet. But the Dalai Lama and Panchen Erdeni held different opinions on the number of delegates. The Dalai Lama requested to send all delegates assigned by his party, while Panchen Erdeni requested to equally divide the number between both parties. After mediation by the Commission for Mongolian and Tibetan Affairs, the Dalai Lama sent six delegates including Gungjor Zongnyi and three non-voting delegates including Curchen Nyima, while the Panchen Erdeni sent four delegates including Lobsang Curchen and five non-voting delegates including Shao Zhang. The 9th Panchen Erdeni also attended the conference and made a significant speech declaring that "Tibet Is Part of Chinese Territory". He not only affirmed by historical fact that Tibet is part of the Chinese territory but also hoped that Tibet could be reconverted to a normal subject relationship with the central government and all nationalities in China could be united to fight against imperialist aggression. In July, the Nationalist Government granted an honorific title to the 9th Panchen Erdeni and offered him jade sheets of confirmation and jade seal of authority.

In December 1932, the Nationalist Government invited him to come to Nanjing again, formally granted him the title of Tibetan Preaching Envoy, and held talks with him on Tibetan affairs. In April 1933, the 9th Panchen sent Living Buddha Anqen and others to Lhasa to meet with the Dalai Lama. The Dalai Lama welcomed the Panchen's return to Tibet and promised to return all his originally held territory. But, before these measures could be carried out, the 13th Dalai Lama died of illness on the 30th day of the 10th Tibetan month in 1933. As usual, the Tibetan government telegraphed to the Nationalist Government and notified the 9th Panchen Erdeni. The Nationalist Government issued the order of granting posthumous title to the 13th Dalai Lama and held the funeral ceremony in Nanjing. The Panchen went to Nanjing from Inner Mongolia as soon as possible to attend the funeral ceremony and served as the committee member of the Nationalist Government.

XIII. The Search and Confirmation of the 14th Dalai Lama

After the 13th Dalai Lama died, the Gaxag government telegraphed to the Nationalist Government in Nanjing and notified the 9th Panchen Erdeni of the fact. Soon after, the ruling group of Tibet changed greatly in their struggle for power. At a conference held by the representatives of the three major monasteries and other monastery and lay officials, Charong

Dasang Zhamdong was deprived of the post of Galoon official and Lungshag was deprived of his post as general of Tibetan army. Gungpeila, one of the favorites of the 13th Dalai Lama, was arrested. So the British-oriented forces in Tibet suffered a heavy shock. According to the system during the Qing Dynasty, Living Buddha Razheng Gyiangbai Yexei Dainzin Gyaincain (1910-1947) took the position of Regent and Langdun Gunggar Wangqug, a relative of the 13th Dalai Lama, took the position of Silun, that is Chief Galoon official in charge of government affairs. After receiving the report from Tibet, the Nationalist Government agreed that Razheng should serve as Regent and assigned Huang Musong as special envoy to travel to Lhasa via the Kham area in order to participate in the mourning and hold negotiations with the local govern-

Regent Living Buddha Razheng was charged with searching the soul boy of the 13th Dalai Lama.
DIMO DAIZIN GYAMCO

ment of Tibet on re-establishing the former close relationship between the two sides. Huang Musong, representing the Nationalist Government, also granted Living Buddha Razheng the honorific title. When Huang Musong departed from Tibet, he left some attendants in Lhasa after winning the agreement for this from the government of Tibet. They served as the organization to reconnect Tibet with the central government under the name of special envoys. When Britain found that the relationship between the government of Tibet and central government was going to improve, they became very restless. They sent some officials to Lhasa to establish a branch office with the approval of the government of Tibet. The Gaxag government also granted Raonong Badu, also known as Norbu Toizhub, a native of Sikkim on the British staff in the branch office, the title of Zhasa. This would enable him to take part in various celebration activities to watch the comings-and-goings between Gaxag government offices and the staff of the Nationalist Government office in Lhasa.

At the same time, Regent Living Buddha Razheng and the Gaxag government started to search for the soul boy of the 13th Dalai Lama. In

Lhamo Toinzhu (front) and his parents and young brother.
GYAMCO

the summer of 1935, Razheng, accompanied by Galoon officials Chimoin Norbu Wanggyi and Kamzhong Rangba Tubdain Gungqen, went the Jokhang and Rampoche monasteries to pray for success in finding the soul boy. They went to to worship at Lhamola Co Lake close to Qoikegyi Monastery and to observe the reflections in the lake waters. Living Buddha Razheng and his attendants put up a temporary tent and preached and prayed to the Mountain Gods with the accompaniment of the Buddhist music played by the lamas of Namgyi Zhacang. It is said that Razheng and Galoon officials rode yaks to the lakefront. Living Buddha Razheng went around the lake three times. On the first occasion, he went with all his attendants formally; but only a few attendants accompanied him on the second and third occasions. Galoon officials also worshipped at the lake for two or three times. They tried to find some omen and vision, but no one saw anything in the

^^ 1)   The Nationalist Government issued a decree on matters concerning the confirmation of Lhamo Toinzhub as the soul boy of the 13th Dalai Lama.

CHEN ZONTGLIE

2)   Decree of the N;ationalist Government on earmarking 400,000 silver dollars to finance the enthronement ceremony.   *CHEN ZONTGLIE*

3)   Decree of the Nationalist Government on sending Wu Zhongxin to Lhasa for the enthronement ceremony as the special envoy of the Nationalist Government.

CHEN ZONTGLIE

lake waters, except for Living Buddha Razheng. He reported to the Commission for Mongolian and Tibetan Affairs that "when searching for the soul boy of 13th Dalai Lama, we could see the vision of his parents and house clearly in the Qoikegyi Lake. We also made nothing of hardships to go to the Qoikegyi Lake and observe the reflections. As a result, I saw the three Tibetan letters of Nga, Gar and Ma in addition to the birth house and the surrounding environment.î In the summer of 1936, Razheng held the "people's conferenceî and repeated to those present that he saw the three Tibetan letters of *Nga, Gar* and *Ma*, a monastery with three layers of Songer gem roof and a golden-tower roof, and a zigzag alley to the east of the monastery leading to a single-story house with a blue roof sitting on a bare mountain. The first Tibetan letter *Nga* represents *Amdo*, referring to the Qinghai area. This tallied with the northeast turning direction of the Dalai Lamaís remains and the direction of the hada scarves cast by every Buddhist Guardian. Acting on the reflections observed in the lake waters, three teams of people went to Qinghai, Xikang and southern Tibet separately to search for the soul boy. In the fifth lunar

<< *The 14th Dalai Lama was enthroned according to the set rituals and historical precedence.*
GYAMCO

∧∧ *The 14th Dalai Lama cabled chairman Lin Seng of the Central Government expressing his thanks to the Central Government care.*
CHEN ZONTGLIE

month of 1937, Living Buddha Jicang, who went to Qinghai, asked the 9th Panchen Erdeni at Yushu to offer the birthplace and the name of the soul boy. He, in turn, offered three choices. In 1938, the people who went to Qinghai found a boy named Lhamo Toinzhub, son of the farmer Qiqu Cerang living in Qijiachuan in Huangzhong and brought him to the Tar Monastery in Qinghai as the soul boy candidate. In the seventh Tibetan month of 1938, Tibet Regent Razheng and the Gaxag government telegraphed to the Tibetan branch office in Chongqing and asked them to go to the Nationalist Government and arrange an escort for the Qinghai soul

Collective picture of officials with the Nationalist Government officice in Tibet,
father of the 14ᵗʰ Dalai Lama, and officials of the local government of Tibet.
Courtesy of CHEN NAIWEN

boy to travel to Tibet for recognition. The telegram said that "in regard to the 13ᵗʰ Dalai Lama's soul boy, two intelligent children have been found in Tibet and one in the Tar Monastery in Xining, Qinghai. According to the traditional rules, the sitting-in-the-bed ceremony must be held after the recognition made by the Buddhist Guardian and Living Buddha. The two children in Tibet are going to be invited. You must go to the Nationalist Government and report the above-mentioned situation, then ask for the approval of inviting the child in the Tar Monastery in Xining, Qinghai. Anything related to the instructions from the Nationalist Government must be reported to us and Living Buddha Gecang." On September

22, 1938, Ngawang Sandain, Gedain Kedain and Tubdain Sanggyi, the Tibetan delegates in the branch office in Nanjing, telegraphed to the Commission for Mongolian and Tibetan Affairs that the soul boy had been found and they asked for the central government's approval to send the soul boy to Tibet to attend the lot-drawing ceremony.

The commission felt this was a significant matter. The method of lot-drawing for confirming the 14th Dalai Lama would be worked out on October 8, 1938 according to the stipulations of the Methods Concerning Soul Boys of Lamas.

In July 1954 the 14th Dalai Lama and the 10th Panchen Erdeni attended the First NPC of the People's Republic of China. The 14th Dalai Lama was elected vice-chairman of the NPC Standing Committee. Pictured here is th 14th Dalai Lama casting his vote.

XIN HUA

As usual, the Tibetan government had reported various things related to the search for the 14th Dalai Lama, and when the lot-drawing ceremony was held in the Jokhang Monastery in Tibet for confirming the soul boy, the High Commissioners had to attend.

Based on three principles, that is, first, the central government would not give up its original rights on Tibet; secondly, unsolved political issues between the central government and Tibetan government would be suspended; and thirdly, all the unsolved cases in recent years should be adjusted to eliminate doubts, explain misunderstandings, harmonize bilateral emotions and strengthen cooperation, the commission worked out

>>
In September of 1954 Chairman Mao received the 14th Dalai Lama (right) and the 10th Panchen Erdeni in Zhongnanhai, site of the PRC Government. XIN HUA

. . . .

three methods: first, the Nationalist Government would send a major official to Lhasa for the lot-drawing ceremony with Razheng Hutogtu; secondly, this major official could assign a representative to deal with this matter for convenience; thirdly, the Nationalist Government would send the leader of Commission for Mongolian and Tibetan Affairs to hold the lot-drawing ceremony with Razheng Hutogtu, and this leader could assign his representative to deal with this matter. The Nationalist Government Executive Yuan answered after studying the report prepared by Commission for Mongolian and Tibetan Affairs that ithis is a very important matter. The Commission for Mongolian and Tibetan Affairs must hold discussions with Tibetan government before handing in this report for ratification.î

On December 18, 1938, the Tibetan branch office in Nanjing handed over the telegram received from the Tibetan government saying that they would receive the leader of the Commission for Mongolian and Tibetan Affairs to hold the ceremony. The telegram said: "We have made a decision to accept the third article in the methods concerning the Dalai Lama soul boy lot-drawing, that is, the leader of Commission for Mongolian and Tibetan Affairs can assign his local representative to deal with this matter. For maintaining the increasingly friendly relations between the Tibetan government and the central government, we would like to accept this method." The Nationalist Government announced an order on December 28, 1938 that, "Wu Zhongxin, leader of the Commission for Mongolian and Tibetan Affairs, is assigned to meet with Razheng Hutogtu and hold the ceremony related to the 14th Dalai Lama soul boy." This order was transmitted to the local government of Tibet, and the latter immediately sent its acceptance. But the monasteries and Living Buddha in Qinghai requested that the soul boy there remain and wait for a while until the central government delegate came to Tibet to hold the lot-drawing ceremony. In addition, the Qinghai Government made it difficult for the soul boy to set off.

After negotiations were held repeatedly between the Nationalist Government and Qinghai province and between the Tibet Regent and the Gaxag government, in July 1939, Ma Bufang, Chairman of Qinghai province, assigned Ma Yunhai, divisional commander, as the special envoy to escort the Qinghai soul boy to Tibet. At the same time, the Nationalist Government sent Wu Zhongxin, leader of the Commission for Mongolian and Tibetan Affairs, to Tibet to meet with Razheng Hutogtu and hold the ceremonies related to the 13th Dalai Lamaís soul boy.

In October 1939, Lhamo Toinzhub arrived in Lhasa. On October 3, Ma Bufang telegraphed to the Commission for Mongolian and Tibetan Affairs that he had escorted the soul boy safely to Razheng Mansion in the eighth lunar month and they were welcomed by people from all fields in Lhasa. But, Wu Zhongxin, leader of the Commission for Mongolian and Tibetan Affairs, could not set off for Tibet through India by sea due to the troubles made by British until early in October. Although several parties made intercessions, the British did not give a transit visa to Wu Zhongxin until the Qinghai soul boy had already arrived in Lhasa. When

^ *In February of 1955, Mao Zedong, Liu Shaoqi and Zhou Enlai met with the 14th Dalai Lama and the10th Panchen Erdeni, wishing them happy Tibet Year of the Wood Sheep.*
XIN HUA

Wu arrived in Lhasa on January 15 1940, therefore, he found that only the Qinghai soul boy remained instead of the three soul boy candidates he expected. Moreover, Regent Living Buddha Razheng had shaved the soul boy's hair and given him the name of Gyizun Jambai Ngawang Lobsang Yexei Dainzin Yamco Sesum Wangqug following Bamai Baide Besangbo, which was usually called Dainzin Yamco. Razheng told Wu: "The Qinghai soul boy is particularly intelligent beyond others. All monasteries and common people in Tibet think he is the soul boy of the 13th Dalai Lama. According to the decision made by the people's conference, the lot-drawing ceremony will not be held. We would like to ask for the exemption of the lot-drawing ceremony following the example of the 13th Dalai Lama." Wu replied: "This issue should be reported to the central government for review. What I can do is to transmit your intention instead of making a decision." Later, the officials of both sides held repeated negotiations until they reached agreement on the exemption of the lot-drawing ceremony with two preconditions: first, Wu Zhongxin must observe by himself the soul boy to see whether he was intelligent or not; secondly, Living Buddha Razheng must write a formal document to the central government asking for exemption from the lot-drawing ceremony. Living Buddha Razheng accepted both preconditions. He handed the required document to Wu on January 26 1940 and asked him to transmit it to the central government. Wu telegraphed to the Nationalist Government after observing the soul boy with the approval of Razheng. But as "the original document is too long to be included in this telegram, there will be another supplementary file for complete statement." At first, he sent a confidential telegram on January 28 1940 to ask the central government to approve the exemption of the lot-drawing ceremony. It said: "According to the report written by Regent Razheng Hutogtu, they had observed the reflections in the lake waters, begged for the visit of the deities and held the monasteries, officials and peopleís conference. They all think the Qinghai soul boy Lhamo Toinzhub is very intelligent and is really the soul boy of the 13th Dalai Lama. So, they asked for the exemption of the lot-drawing ceremony and the hair-shaving ceremony would be held as tradition rules, which had been reported to the central government. So, the sitting-in-the-bed ceremony will be held on the 14th day of the first Tibetan month, that is the 24th day of February, (note: it is February 22 in fact). I have observed the soul boy and am sure that he is really intelligent. So, I beg the Nationalist Government to approve the succession of the soul boy Lhamo Toinzhub to the position of the 14th Dalai Lama so that they can prepare the sitting-in-the-bed ceremony in time." On February 5, the Nationalist Government issued the order to exempt the lot-drawing ceremony and permit Qinghai soul boy Lhamo Toinzhub to succeed as the 14th Dalai Lama. The following is the details of the order:

"Qinghai soul boy Lhamo Toinzhub is particularly intelligent and is testified as the 13th Dalai Lamaís soul boy. So, the lot-drawing ceremony shall be exempted with approval and he is permitted to succeed the 14th Dalai Lama."

"According to this special order, Lhamo Toinzhub is permitted to succeed as the 14th Dalai Lama and the Executive Yuan will allocate 400,000 silver dollars from Financial Ministry for the sitting-in-the-bed ceremony. The Republic of China February 5,1940."

On February 22, the sitting-in-the-bed ceremony was held in Potala Palace according to the traditional rules. At that time, British government also sent Gude, Sikkim Chief Minister, to Lhasa under the pretense of watching the ceremony. Gude instigated the Gaxag government to place the seat of Wu Zhongxin opposite Razheng with the same grade as Silun and to place the seat of Gude beside Wu Zhongxin. Due to the formal request made by Wu, the Gaxag government had to give up this idea and placed the seat of Wu beside Dalai Lama with the same grade; Gude did not attend the sitting-in-the-bed ceremony of the 14th Dalai Lama because he could not get the seating position he wanted.

Postscript

To sum up, the search and confirmation of the soul boy of a late Dalai Lama or a late Living Buddha has gradually developed into a pattern after hundreds of years of constant development. The central government of Qing Dynasty played a role in developing the pattern into historical precedence. According to this, the search and confirmation of the soul boy of a late Dalai Lama is divided into three major steps, that is, search, confirmation and sitting-in-the-bed ceremony.

1. Searching a soul boy includes four major procedures.

Firstly, examine the speech and deportment and omens of the late Dalai Lama before death, his will, and the omens after he died, and then organize the searching staff. According to the *Biography of the 7th Dalai Lama,* when the 6th Dalai Lama Cangyang Gyamco was going to be escorted to Beijing, thousands of disciples begged his eternal blessing. At that time, a piece of white *hada* scarf blew in the wind in front of him. It flew away again and landed on top of the Potala Palace, although some said it was within the city. It was said to be the omen indicating the Dalai Lama would stay in the Han's area for a while and the soul boy would return to Tibet soon. After Cangyang Gyamco died in Gungar Nor, and his remains were brought to Xining. During the cremation ceremony, a cloud rose from the cremated remains and drifted south. It was regarded as confirming the saying that the 7th Dalai Lama was born in southern Xining. In addition, Cangyang Gyamco once sang a song, *The white crane flies in the sky by use of my wings; I will go away and be reincarnated in Litang.* So people thought it indicated his soul boy would come from Litang.

Also, according to *Biography of the 12th Dalai Lama*, the 12th Dalai Lama Chilai Gyamco died facing the southeast, and after his remains were moved to the mourning hall facing south, they reverted automatically to the southeast, which indicated that the soul boy would be born in that direction. After the 13th Dalai Lama died, many odd clouds appeared in the northeastern sky. There is another saying that his disciples made a fire on the roof and the smoke blew away to the northeast. It was recorded in Tibetan historical documents that the remains of the Dalai, although placed facing south on the throne in Norbu Lingka, turned to the east without being touched. Later, a star-like mushroom grew beside a pillar in the northeast of the holy stupa of the 13th Dalai Lama in addition to other good omens. All of these omens indicated the birthplace of the soul boy. Then, the searching staff was organized. It was usually the Regent who assembled his favorites and divided them into several groups to make search.

Secondly, according to the omens appearing before or after the death of the late Dalai Lama, the local government of Tibet and three major monasteries organized some eminent Living Buddha to cast lots and asked the Buddhist Guardian to observe the reflections in the holy Lake. At last, the direction of the birthplace, routine and local character would be confirmed by integrating all these results.

Casting lots is a traditional Buddhist activity. According to some historical documents, during the Tubo period, casting lots was very popular in Buddhist fields. It was recorded in *Record of Tibet*: "There are various methods of casting lots. Some lamas painted the Eight Diagrams on paper and wrote down Fan character for divination. Some lamas ranged *qingke* barley in the shape of the Eight Diagrams and took out colorful wool for divination. Some counted white bead for divination. Others painted on the ground or burned goat bones, or observe small bowls for divination."

Since the rise of the Gelug Sect, casting lots has been regarded as one Buddhist activity in presuming the direction of the birthplace of the soul boy of the late Living Buddha. When the 7th Dalai Lama died, the 6th

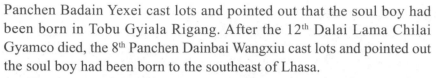

Panchen Badain Yexei cast lots and pointed out that the soul boy had been born in Tobu Gyiala Rigang. After the 12th Dalai Lama Chilai Gyamco died, the 8th Panchen Dainbai Wangxiu cast lots and pointed out the soul boy had been born to the southeast of Lhasa.

The descent of Chuizhong was once the most important activity during the searching for a soul boy. Chuizhong originated from Tibetan and is the Mandarin pronunciation of the Buddhist Guardian. God descending activity started from Tubo period. After the rise of the Gelug Sect, much attention was paid to the Buddhist Guardian, for whom special lamas appeared. According to the *Record of Tibet*: "The Chuizhong Hall, with the traditional name of Garmaxia, is half a mile from Jokhang Monastery in the east. The statues of God in the hall looked very ferocious. The Buddhist Guardian lived in the hall. He dressed in lamaís costume and married and had children. He passed down his magic to descendants and belonged to the Chinese wizards. On the 26th day of each lunar month, Deity descended. He would wear a golden helmet with a hank of chicken feather some two or three feet long. He would also wear armor with five flags on the back. He was wrapped in white *hada* scarves from head to foot, with tiger-skinned boots on his feet and a bowed sword in the hand. Common people would ask him about good or ill luck and he would make a judgment by the words of God.

During the Qing Dynasty, four monasteries of the Gelug Sect were determined to have Buddhist Guardians. They were:

1) Lhamo Monastery, which is located in the region of modern Darze County;

2) Nequn Monastery, which is located at the foot of the mountains southeast to the Zhaibung Monastery in Lhasa;

3) Gardong Monastery, which is located not far away from northwest of the Zhaibung Monastery in Lhasa;

4) Samye Monastery, which is located in Zhanang County in Shannan.

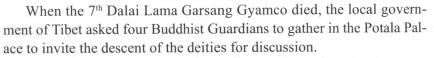

When the 7th Dalai Lama Garsang Gyamco died, the local government of Tibet asked four Buddhist Guardians to gather in the Potala Palace to invite the descent of the deities for discussion.

But when the 12th Dalai Lama Chilai Gyamco died, the local government of Tibet asked the Samye Monastery in Shannan to invite deities who showed that the soul boy of the late Dalai Lama was born in the southeastern place. Later, some fraudulent practices were carried on as recorded in the appendix of Religious Source of Tibet, "some did fraudulent practices deliberately, some did so to favor his relatives, and others were directed by the Dalai Lama or Panchen Erdeni stealthily to make identification."

With regard to this situation, Emperor Qianlong made a decision to carry on the lot-drawing ceremony to strengthen the control and management of the search of the soul boy of the late Living Buddha.

Observing the holy lake for reflections is also a major procedure of searching and confirming the soul boy of the late Dalai Lama. Within the area of Gyacha County in Shannan, Tibet, there is Lhamola Co Lake, which is also called Qoikegyi Lake. It is on top of a mountain with many shadows and so is regarded as the God Lake with the highest and mightiest authority. According to Tibetan historical documents, the Gelug Sect viewed Lhamola Co Lake as the soul lake of the goddess of luck. The 2nd Dalai Lama Gendun Gyamco built Qoikegyi Monastery not far from the Lake. According to Ya Han-zhangís Biography of the Panchen Erdeni, the 4th Dalai Lama Yundain Gyamco invited the 4th Panchen to worship at Lhamola Co Lake in 1604. The 5th Dalai Lama once observed the lake for omens prior to journeying to Beijing. According to the *Biography of the 5th Dalai Lama*, the 5th Dalai Lama once saw a city of heavy traffic in the Lake, and this indicated that he would go to the hinterland to meet the Emperor.

According to the historical documents, observing the holy lake for reflections to search for the soul boy of the late Dalai Lama started from the search for the 12ᵗʰ Dalai Lama's soul boy. It is recorded in *Biography of the 13ᵗʰ Dalai Lama-Gems* that after the 12ᵗʰ Dalai Lama died in 1875, in September 1876, for getting the information about the birthplace and the family character of the soul boy, Lobsang Dagyi, who had left his position of abbot in the Upper Tantric School, went with attendants to Lhamola Co Lake. They cast *hada* scarves, treasure bottles and medicinal materials in the Lake and prayed. Lobsang Dagyi got the information from the reflections he saw in the lake that a boy was born in a farmerís family in Langdun Village, Darbu Region, southeast of Lhasa. Then they went there to check.

According to Tibetan historical documents, when the 13ᵗʰ Dalai Lama died in1933, as usual, in May 1935, Regent Living Buddha Razheng, Galoon officials Chimoin, Norbu Wanggyi, Kamzhong Zhaxi Lingba, Qenrao Wangqug, Rangba and Dadain Gungqen went to Gyimai Dutang Monastery, that is Qoikegyi Monastery, to sacrifice to the Buddhist Guardian Deities with the Lucky Goddess as the chief. Then, Razheng Regent went to the Goddess Soul Lake, that is Lhamola Co Lake, above the monastery to observe the reflections in its waters. He wrote down what he saw: "A Tibetan character, *Nga*, appeared in the lake, and there then appeared a three-story monastery which was covered with glazed tiles on the middle story and by gilded copper tiles on the top story. North of the monastery, there is an alley leading to a hill. Beside the hill, there is a house with a pine as its top decoration and this is the home of the 14ᵗʰ Dalai Lama." Based on this, the local government of Tibet sent three groups to search for the soul boy in three different directions.

After confirming the direction of the birthplace and the local character of the soul boy, some eminent lamas would be organized to lead a group to search for intelligent children. No matter how many children would be found, they should observe their speech and deportment, body

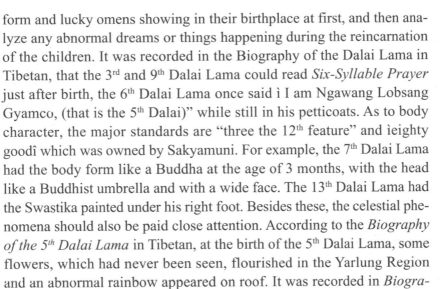

form and lucky omens showing in their birthplace at first, and then analyze any abnormal dreams or things happening during the reincarnation of the children. It was recorded in the Biography of the Dalai Lama in Tibetan, that the 3rd and 9th Dalai Lama could read *Six-Syllable Prayer* just after birth, the 6th Dalai Lama once said ì I am Ngawang Lobsang Gyamco, (that is the 5th Dalai)" while still in his petticoats. As to body character, the major standards are "three the 12th feature" and ìeighty goodî which was owned by Sakyamuni. For example, the 7th Dalai Lama had the body form like a Buddha at the age of 3 months, with the head like a Buddhist umbrella and with a wide face. The 13th Dalai Lama had the Swastika painted under his right foot. Besides these, the celestial phenomena should also be paid close attention. According to the *Biography of the 5th Dalai Lama* in Tibetan, at the birth of the 5th Dalai Lama, some flowers, which had never been seen, flourished in the Yarlung Region and an abnormal rainbow appeared on roof. It was recorded in *Biography of the 7th Dalai Lama* in Tibetan that at his birth, there was a rainbow almost covering the whole sky as well as the continuous thunder. All of these things are viewed as good omens in children.

Fourthly, identifying the relic. This lets the soul boy candidates identify relics of the late Dalai Lama, such as prayer beads, tambourine, bell pestle, walking stick and bowl, from among other articles of the same shape. If a soul boy candidate can recognize the relic, he will be proved to be the real soul boy of the late Dalai Lama. It must be the monasteries with high prestige or the close servants of the late Dalai Lama who lead the soul boy candidates to identify the relics. According to Biography of *the 6th Dalai Lama-Golden Tassels* in Tibetan, in order to test the soul boy candidates, Diba Sanggyi Gyamco assigned Kariba Soinam Dorje and Soigyam to go to Cona with the Buddhist figures and the articles the 5th Dalai Lama once used and some imitation items. They tested the soul boy candidate for seven days and found he could correctly identify all the relics. After that, Diba Sanggyi Gyamco always sent persons to take care of soul boy candidates. According to Biography of the 8th Dalai Lama-Adornments of the World in Tibetan, Zanggyia Hotogtu Rubi Dorje came back from Beijing immediately and cast lots as the representative of the Regent Normen Khan and other honorable lamas, Living Buddhas, the Lhamo Monastery Buddhist Guardian, the Nequn Monastery Buddhist Guardian, and Samye Buddhist Guardian. He identified the three children in the Kham, Xigaze and Oiga areas respectively as the soul boy candidates. Then, some persons were sent to these places with the relics of the 7th Dalai Lama to make an investigation. They came back with the report that the child born in Togyi Lharigang on the 15th day of the sixth lunar month of 1758 had kind features. For the second time, handlers of miscellaneous affairs Zhaba Taya, Zongye Yundain Lezhub, and Zeben Walawa went to Togyi Lharigang with the original and copies of the Buddhist figures, articles and clothes of the 7th Dalai Lama for testing the child. The child made an accurate identification and was confirmed as the soul boy candidate. According to *Biography of the 11th Dalai Lama-Music From the Heaven* in Tibetan, in the fifth lunar month of 1841, the 7th Panchen Dainbai Nyima, Regent Normenkhan, the two High Commissioners, sutra teachers of the three major monasteries, Living Buddha, executive monasteries and Galoon officials went to Daqen Sang'aka Monastery to meet the three chosen children and let them identify the Buddhist figures and articles of late Dalai Lama and they all made an accurate identification. So all the three children took part in the lot-drawing ceremony as soul boy candidates.

With the completion of the four procedures aforementioned, the search could move on to the beginning of the confirmation stage. The soul boy candidates cannot be called as soul boys until the conclusion of the confirmation stage. Before the holding of the sitting-in-the-bed ceremony, he will always be called soul boy.

2. Confirm the soul boy:

Since the confirmation of the 5th Dalai Lama Ngawang Lobsang Gyamco, the confirmation of each Dalai Lama needed ratification of the central government. After the 5th Dalai Lama, the confirmation procedures of each Dalai Lama included two stages, that is the local government of Tibet and monastery group finished the search procedures and handed a confirmed soul boy candidate over to the central government for getting approval or titles. The detailed procedures were to write down the information of the confirmed soul boy, send someone to Beijing or let the staff sent by Emperor for viewing the soul boy go back to Beijing with a report, and then Emperor sent down the imperial edict of approval with the formal confirmation. According to *Biography of Zanggyia Rubi Dorje* and *Biography of the 8th Dalai Lama:Adornments of the World* in Tibetan, in 1760 Zanggyia Hotogtu sent by Emperor Qianlong for the search returned to Beijing and reported all the information about the confirmed soul boy to the Emperor. Then, Emperor Qianlong sent down the imperial edict: "The child from Xigaze area has been confirmed as the Dalai Lama's soul boy and he can be invited to the place near the Potala Palace without disturbance to wait for the sitting-in-the-bed ceremony." Following the imperial edict, Regent Living Buddha Dimo, Minister Jishan, Noryun Gongban Dida and their attendants went to the Xigaze area to invite the soul boy to Lhasa. After the 29-Article Ordinance was issued, the lot-drawing ceremony also had to be carried out during the confirmation of Dalai Lama and the Panchen Erdeni; exemption needed central government approval.

The 10th, the 11th and the 12th Dalai Lama followed these procedures during the confirmation. But for the 9th, 13th and 14th Dalai Lama, as only one intelligent child was found, the lot-drawing ceremony was exempted with the approval of the central government at the request of deputies of the High Commissioners, the Nationalist Government Commission for

Mongolian and Tibetan Affairs, the Regent and other Hotogtu.

The lot-drawing ceremony is of significant political meaning that the power of deciding the successor of Dalai Lama and Panchen belonged to the central government. After the lot-drawing ceremony was carried out, it was exempted in some cases. But the power of deciding ìexemptionî or ìno exemptionî also belonged to the central government and the Emperor. The local government of Tibet had no other right than that of requisition.

3. Sitting-in-the-bed Ceremony

After the strict confirmation procedures, one of the soul boy candidates became the soul boy. Then, it should be reported to the central government for approval of holding the sitting-in-the-bed ceremony. The holding of the sitting-in-the-bed ceremony signified the formal enthronement of a new Dalai Lama. The sitting-in-the-bed ceremony always included three procedures.

First was to declare the imperial edict to the soul boy. According to *Biography of the 10th Dalai Lama*, "In the fourth lunar month, the 7th Panchen, Regent Normenkhan, two High Commissioners and other Tibetan or Han's officials and eminent monks went to Dewagyian Monastery in Nytang Rewadui. After all assembled in the Grand Sutra Hall, the soul boy sat on a mat and kowtowed to the east while Zongye Yukang and Gyiangbai Deleg read the imperial edict. Later, everyone in the Hall bent their knees three times and kowtowed nine times for worshiping the Emperor."

Secondly, eminent monks were invited to shave the hair of the soul boy and grant him with the cassock and Buddhist title. It was always Panchen who shaved the hair of the Dalai Lama's soul boy. The 5th, 6th, 7th, 8th, 9th, 10th, 11th and 13th Dalai Lamas was shaved and granted the cassock and Buddhist title by Panchen of that time, with the exception of the 12th and 14th Dalai Lama. At the time of confirming the 12th Dalai Lamaís soul boy, the 7th Panchen had died and the 8th Panchen was only four years old so he could not shave the hair of Dalai Lama's soul boy or grant him the title. Hence, it was Razheng Hotogtu who did these things. At the time of confirming the 14th Dalai Lama, the 9th Panchen had not returned to Tibet from the hinterland, so it was Regent Razheng Hotogtu who performed the rite.

Thirdly, select the lucky date of holding the sitting-in-the-bed ceremony. Since the 6th Dalai Lama, the Potala Palace was the location of the ceremony. According to Han or Tibetan historical documents, the sitting-in-the-bed ceremony was not held before the 2nd Dalai Lama. The 4th and 5th Dalai Lama held their sitting-in-the-bed ceremony in Razheng Monastery and the Zhaibung Monastery. When holding the sitting-in-the-bed ceremony, Emperor would grant golden sheets of confirmation and golden seal of authority. The Emperor sent ministers to Tibet for viewing or asked the High Commissioners to deal with these issues. The attendants of the sitting-in-the-bed ceremony always included Panchen, Gaxag government members, deputies of three major monasteries, eminent Living Buddha and Hotogtu in addition to imperial ministers. Moreover, deputies of Nepal, Kashmir and other neighboring countries and regions also took part in the ceremony. When holding the sitting-in-the-bed ceremony of the 14th Dalai Lama, the Nationalist Government sent Wu Zhongxin, Chief of Commission for Mongolian and Tibetan Affairs, to hold the sitting-in-the-bed ceremony. But at the instigation of British imperialists, some persons in the upper class of the local government of Tibet and some pro-British persons stirred up dissension with Wu Zhongxin. But Wu did not give up in many fundamental issues and maintained the unity of the country and authority of the central government. The sitting-in-the-bed ceremony was held according to the scheduled procedures.

With this step, the procedures of searching and confirming Dalai Lamaís soul boy are concluded. A new Dalai Lama ascends to throne formally.

History indicates that the formalization of the historical precedence of the soul boy of a late Dalai Lama or a late Living Buddha existed in order to maintain the social stability and avoid conflicts and war that happened during the confirmation of the 6th and the 7th Dalai Lama. After the formalization, the historical precedence was carried on in most cases. Even in the period of the Republic of China when relations between the local government of Tibet and the central government were not normal, the search, confirmation and sitting-in-the-bed ceremony of the 14th Dalai Lama followed the historical precedence basically. The confirmation and sitting-in-the-bed ceremony procedures were concluded successfully with the attendance of the central governmentís official and the approval of exempting the lot-drawing ceremony by the central government. These historical facts were recorded in many Tibetan or Chinese historical documents and the description files of persons related, which cannot be denied by anyone.

Today, in accordance with the facts in Tibet, the central government agreed to carry on the Tibetan Buddhism ceremonies related to Living Buddha soul boy. This shows respect to Tibetan tradition as well as to Buddhism belief and Buddhism emotion of Tibetan people. Confirming Living Buddhaís soul boy can be carried on successfully only by sticking to historical precedence. Any divergence would result in disturbance and chaos. So, perseverance of the historical precedence with regard to the incarnation of the Dalai Lama or Living Buddha can help maintain the unity of the country and the comity among all nationalities and Tibetan people as well as the social stability and economic development in Tibet. It is therefore the significant principles that we should persevere with.

图书在版编目 (CIP)数据

达赖喇嘛转世／陈庆英著；王国振译.
－北京：五洲传播出版社，2005.7
ISBN 7-5085-0745-2

Ⅰ.达…　Ⅱ.①陈…②王…　Ⅲ.喇嘛教－制度－英文
Ⅳ.B946.6
中国版本图书馆 CIP 数据核字(2005) 第 073910 号

《达赖喇嘛转世》
特约编辑：张晓明
责任编辑：荆孝敏
编辑助理：李卫锋
英文翻译：王国振
设计制版：北京永乐时代营销策划有限公司
印　　刷：北京彩艺嘉禾印刷有限公司

《达赖喇嘛转世》
五洲传播出版社

地址：中国北京海淀区莲花池东路北小马厂 6 号
邮编：100038
电话：58891280　　网址：www.cicc.org.cn

开本：140 × 210　1/32　印张：5
2005 年 7 月第一版　印数 1-5100
ISBN 7-5085-0745-2/B·50
定价：48.00 元